Britain in Palestine

A unique photographic archive used throughout this book shows life in Palestine between 1898 and 1946. All we know about this picture is that it features an anonymous Palestinian woman.

Britain in Palestine

The Story of British Rule in Palestine, 1917–48

by Karl Sabbagh

based on the exhibition
Britain in Palestine
by Anne Lineen

SKYSCRAPER PUBLICATIONS

Published by Skyscraper Publications
skyscraper.books@btinternet.com

First published by Skyscraper Publications 2012

Typeset by Bookcraft Ltd, Stroud, UK
Printed and bound by CPI Group (UK) Ltd, Croydon, CR0 4YY

ISBN: 978-0-9551810-1-6

Contents

Preface

The genesis of this book was an exhibition held at the Brunei Gallery in late 2012, and the book largely follows the narrative of the exhibition, using text, photos and quotes written or gathered by Anne Lineen, the curator, or by me as a consultant to the exhibition. But I have expanded certain sections here and there and so any views expressed may sometimes be mine rather than Anne Lineen's.

The exhibition used interview material filmed over the last few years with a range of Palestinian Arabs, Jews and British people with experience of Palestine during the Mandate period. To simplify the book, I have used quotes from just two of those interviewees, Uri Avnery, a veteran Jewish commentator on Palestine and Israel, and Hazem Nuseibeh, a Palestinian activist and broadcaster during the Mandate period. Both men were born within a year of each other and lived through almost three decades of Mandate Palestine. The quotes from these two interviewees are indicated with a Star of David for Uri Avnery and a crescent symbol for Nuseibeh.

The photographs, including the frontispiece, come from the unique copyright-free Matson collection at the U.S. Library of Congress, and the individual retrieval numbers are given in the list on pp.107–8.

I am extremely grateful to Anne Lineen for providing me with unfettered access to the material she gathered for the exhibition *Britain in Palestine*, held at the Brunei Gallery in London from October to December 2012. I should also like to thank Uri Avnery and Hazem Nuseibeh for making themselves available to Anne Lineen and me for long and detailed interviews about their memories of the British Mandate in Palestine.

Introduction

For many newspaper readers in the twenty-first century, the heart of the Arab-Israeli dispute is seen as the occupation of the West Bank and Gaza, and Israel's treatment of the Palestinians who live there. The implication of this is that if the Israelis left the territories they illegally occupy, and allowed the Palestinians to govern themselves, peace would reign in the Middle East.

But for Palestinians the issue is different. Of course they – and the world – see the Occupation as unjust. But for them, the bigger injustice is what took place between 1917 and 1948, when the Arab country of Palestine was turned into a Jewish state. And the causes of that transformation lay in the actions of the British government before, during and after the First World War.

Whether or not it is realistic to expect – as many Palestinians do – the restitution of Palestine/Israel as a democratic state of all its citizens, no peace agreement will be sustainable unless the Palestinian sense of injustice at the original occupation of Palestine, which took place when Britain was in charge of the country, is taken into account, alongside the later and more extensive occupations of Palestinian territory that have happened since 1948.

This is why an understanding of what took place when Britain sought, drafted and operated the League of Nations Mandate to control Palestine after the First World War is essential to an understanding of the modern conflict between Israel and Palestine. In this short book, based on the detailed research that went into the exhibition *Britain in Palestine,* I have tried to pare down a complex story to clarify the importance of Britain's role in the modern conflict.

1

Palestine before the British

The Land of Palestine

'All chronicles call this country the land of Palestine'

Evliya Çelebi, *Book of Travels*, 1671.

The land on the eastern shores of the Mediterranean was called 'Palestine' from the fifth century BC. The name comes from 'Philistia', the ancient coastal kingdom of the Philistines. Throughout its long history Palestine has seen conquerors, traders, migrations and intermingling of peoples. It is part of the farming region known as the Fertile Crescent, and its Mediterranean ports and overland trading links to Egypt, Arabia and northern Syria have been in use since ancient times. From the sixteenth century to 1917 Palestine was part of the Ottoman Empire and ruled from Constantinople. The north was administered from Beirut, and the south from Jerusalem. The area was still known as Palestine; referred to in official Ottoman documents as the 'Land of Palestine' (*Ard-Filastin*).

The land of Palestine has been inhabited for thousands of years. The peoples of the ancient Canaanite, Israelite and Philistine kingdoms that inhabited the region had been subjugated in turn by the empires of the Assyrians, Babylonians, Persians, Greeks and Romans. Among the groups who arrived and lived among the other Palestinian peoples about 3,000 years ago were a people known as Hebrews who became known as 'Jews' from one of the areas they inhabited, Judaea. Groups of Arab traders and artisans had long travelled through Palestine from the Arabian Peninsula. In the seventh century AD the Arab Islamic armies conquered Palestine and Arabs settled in the country, joining and mixing with the existing population. Over time Arab culture and language, and the religion of Islam, came to dominate the land, although there were also small religious Jewish communities in a few Palestinian towns. Apart from a century of Christian Crusader rule from 1099 to 1187, Palestine was ruled by a series of Muslim kingdoms from the seventh century through to the arrival of the British in 1917.

This succession of rulers and overlords throughout Palestine's history brought new cultures and beliefs, and different systems of government. However, over these thousands of years the people of Palestine continued to farm their land, trade their crops and build their towns and villages.

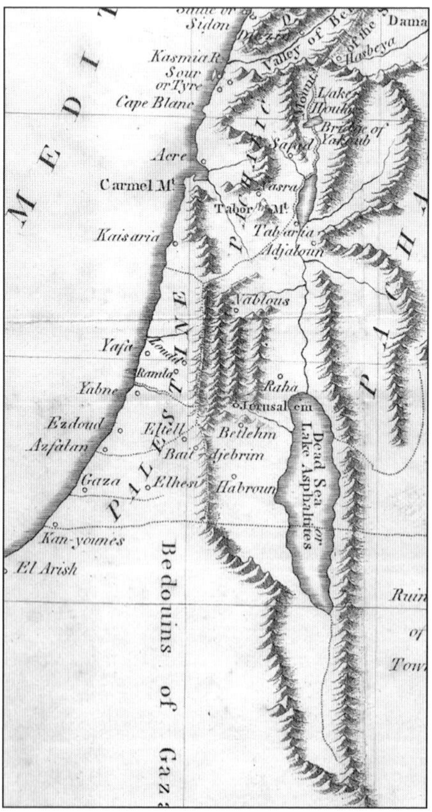

Palestine in the 1780s

THE PEOPLE OF PALESTINE

'The noble Ottoman nation is made up of different groups who live together ... '

SHLOMO YELLIN, JEWISH LAWYER, BEIRUT, 1909.

Although the Ottoman Empire was ruled by an Islamic government, it was home to a multitude of religious and national groups. In Palestine this diversity of belief, language and ethnicity was an accepted part of life. Although Christians and Jews had a different status from the majority Muslim population, there were many places in which Muslims, Christians and Jews lived together in harmony. Even the four cities with the highest proportion of Jews had significant Arab populations.

	Muslims	Christians	Arabs	Jews	% Jews	Total
1860–61	325,000	31,000	356,000	13,000	3.5	369,000
1882–83	408,318	44,471	452,789	15,300	3.3	468,089
1895–96	469,750	58,987	528,737	20,117	3.7	548,854
1905–6	531,236	69,092	600,328	27,862	4.4	628,190
1914–15	602,337	81,012	683,349	38,754	5.4	722,103

Population groups in Palestine, 1860 to 1915[1]

Christians have lived in Palestine for nearly 2,000 years. Christianity was the dominant religion in the region before the development of Islam from the seventh century AD. Christians and Muslims in Palestine share the same Arab culture and language. In Palestine the long-established religious Jewish communities lived in Jerusalem, Safad, Hebron and Tiberias. When Jews were expelled from Spain in 1492 they were offered sanctuary in the Ottoman Empire by the Sultan. These Jews were described as Sephardi and spoke Ladino and Arabic. From the late nineteenth century Orthodox Jews from Eastern Europe, Ashkenazis, came to Palestine to live in the towns. They came for religious reasons, but also because they faced violent persecution in eastern Europe.

POLITICS IN PALESTINE

'... all went forward with one heart to celebrate freedom!'

AMERICAN CONSUL IN PALESTINE, 12TH AUGUST 1908

There were celebrations throughout the Ottoman Empire, including Palestine, when the Committee for Union and Progress (CUP) took control of the Ottoman government in Istanbul from the Sultan in July 1908. The new government promised an era of democracy, freedom and equality. The public discussions that flowed from this event emphasized brotherhood and unity between religious and national groups; loyalty to the Ottoman homeland required all peoples to be active citizens.

In 1908 and 1912 elections to the Ottoman parliament were held throughout the empire, in which all male citizens could vote; Palestine sent five elected representatives to the parliament.

'Let me inform you, O brother, that your homeland Palestine is part of great lands claimed by the Ottoman Empire, and as long as the existence of this empire is preserved, if you send me as a deputy on your behalf its stability and its prestige and the preservation of its possessions will be the first order of importance for me ... '

ELECTION LEAFLET OF SA'ID ABU KHADRA', FROM GAZA, STANDING FOR ELECTION TO THE OTTOMAN PARLIAMENT, 1912.[2]

'Palestine had representatives in Istanbul as members of parliament. They were experienced in the ways of state, and the ways of international politics. The Ottoman Empire was a condominium, so to speak. It had two major sectors: the Turkish and the Arab. The Arab was the Arab world all the way from Istanbul to Algeria. Each city had representatives in the Ottoman parliament, when they started liberalising their regime after Abu Hamid and so on. Those people were at the helm of power, and Istanbul was one of the major capitals

in the world. One of the commanders of the Turkish army, Showqat, was an Iraqi Arab. There was no discrimination, the Arabs were on equal terms with the Turks in managing the empire.'

Hazem Nuseibeh

This period of excitement and hope also brought with it uncertainty, disappointment and group rivalry. Arabs in the Ottoman Empire hoped for a degree of autonomy within the Empire, but in spite of its professed ideals, the new Ottoman government increased central control, and promoted Turkish identity and language.

An additional concern for the people of Palestine was the Zionist movement that was emerging from Europe. Zionism, derived from a Hebrew synonym for Jerusalem, 'Zion', had developed amongst Jews in Russia faced with persecution and violent anti-semitism in the late nineteenth century. It combined European ideas about nationalism with Jewish religious ideas about a return to 'Zion'; some Zionists felt that the colonisation of Palestine by Jews would secure a refuge from persecution and enhance a national Jewish identity. When hundreds of thousands of Jews had to flee Russia from 1882 onwards, the majority went to the United States, but a small minority chose Palestine as their refuge. These Ashkenazi Jews mainly settled in the mixed towns alongside the Muslim, Christian and Jewish Sephardi communities, but some set up separate Zionist farming colonies.

In Palestine, many Palestinian Arabs and even some religious Jews viewed Zionism as a European-sponsored threat that would ultimately change the land and affect the rights of its existing inhabitants. Palestinian Jews did not necessarily support Zionism's political aim of securing a Jewish state, but some did approve of its efforts to revitalize Jewish culture and promote agricultural work, sporting clubs and the Hebrew language. Other Palestinian Jews denounced Zionism as incompatible with Ottoman loyalty.

In the devastation of the First World War, the ideals of the 1908 revolution in the Ottoman Empire would be lost to brutal suppression, Arab nationalism and the triumph of political Zionism.

PALESTINE, THE HOLY LAND

To Jews, Christians and Muslims throughout the world, Palestine is their Holy Land, a place central to the founding of their religion. The holy books of the Old Testament, New Testament and the Qu'ran all describe crucial events and the assertion of essential moral rules that took place in Palestine. Some of the many holy sites and places of worship scattered throughout Palestine are shared and revered by people of all three faiths.

Hebron, for example, is believed by Christians, Muslims and Jews to house the tomb of Abraham, revered by Muslims and Jews as a patriarch and a prophet. The town is known in Arabic as 'al-Khalil', the Friend, after one of Abraham's names, the Friend of God.

The overlapping of religious locations is most prominent in Jerusalem. The Western Wall is significant to Jews as part of the retaining wall for the platform, Temple Mount, on which Herod built his temple in 38–4 BC. This temple was destroyed by the Romans in 70 AD. Jews in Jerusalem began praying at this wall because it was the closest they could get to the original temple site. Gradually the wall itself became a religious and holy site. With the arrival in the nineteenth century of tourists, pilgrims and photography to Jerusalem, the wall became a symbol around the world of the Jewish presence in Jerusalem.

Above the Wall is the Dome of the Rock, a mosque sacred to Muslims. It was built in 691 AD by Caliph Abd al-Malik, and it is a shrine and a place of prayer. The area is known as the Haram al-Sharif, and it also houses the Mosque of al-Aqsa built between 705 and 715 AD by Abd al-Walid, along with shrines, fountains and tombs of Muslim saints and scholars placed there by successive Muslim rulers.

Jerusalem (*al Quds* in Arabic – 'the Holy') is central to Islamic belief. The Qur'an, and a later eighth century biography of the Prophet Mohammad, describe the Prophet's Night Journey from Mecca to Jerusalem where he ascended to heaven from the rock on Temple Mount. The Qur'an also records that in the early years of Islam Muslims were to pray facing towards Jerusalem, in the way that they would later face Mecca.

The Western, or Wailing, Wall in the Old City of Jerusalem

The factors in common between the three faiths are often demonstrated in religious festivals in Palestine. The Nebi Musa festival, for example, was a traditional annual procession to the shrine of the Prophet Moses which was attended by people of all faiths from all over Palestine. All the people of Palestine regarded their whole land as holy, and honoured its sacred sites.

Not far away from the main Jewish and Muslim site of the Temple Mount is the Church of the Holy Sepulchre, on a site which has housed a church since the fourth century, when Christianity became the official religion of the Roman Empire. It is believed to be the site of the crucifixion and burial of Jesus.

The Holy Sepulchre, sacred site to Christians in Jerusalem

PALESTINE'S ECONOMY

'If Hebron could boast of its glass bracelets, its big he-goat skins, and its fine grapes; if Gaza was still the granary of Palestine; if Lydda was reputed for its oil markets and mat industry; Nablus could point with pride to its soap manufactories, one of the most important factors of the wealth of that prosperous inland town.'

HASSAN YASEEN ABU RAZEK, NATIVE OF HEBRON[3]

'Wheat, wheat, a very ocean of wheat.'

W.M. THOMPSON, DESCRIBING THE SOUTHERN COASTAL PLAIN OF PALESTINE IN THE MID-NINETEENTH CENTURY[4]

Although some travellers to the Holy Land in the nineteenth century described it as 'desolate', this is far from the truth. Palestine's economy was based on products of the land, grown around the hundreds of villages scattered throughout the country. The towns developed as centres of trade and culture, and along the Mediterranean coast the ports of Jaffa, Gaza and Acre were linked to a global trading network. Inland trading towns such as Hebron and Nablus were part of the wider economy of the region, producing and exchanging goods through Beirut, Damascus and further afield.

By the end of the nineteenth century Palestine's economy was expanding, the towns were growing and the population was rising. The British Consul in Palestine reported in 1910 that exports from Palestine had increased and that more land was coming under cultivation. He also noted that water pumps for land irrigation were being imported.

The varied landscape of Palestine enabled the farmers (*fellahin*) to grow a wide range of crops: oranges and grapes along the coast, wheat in the southern region and olives in the hill districts.

Reaping the barley harvest in Palestine

In the late nineteenth and early twentieth centuries much of the barley grown in southern Palestine was shipped through the port of Gaza to Britain for the brewing industry.

An additional feature of Palestine's economy was the booming tourist and pilgrim trade that developed from the 1870s. Christian, Muslim and Jewish pilgrims came from all over the world to visit their holy sites in Palestine. These visitors provided work for boatmen, guides, interpreters, souvenir makers, shops and hotels. In Bethlehem and Jerusalem, artisans working in olive wood and shell produced a vast range of souvenirs and religious ornaments for tourists and for export.

Specific towns and villages were known for their crafts. This jewellery store sells blue glass made in Hebron.

Artisans worked in all the towns and villages of Palestine producing useful items such as textiles, pots and agricultural tools.

Olives were an important cash crop in Palestine. Olive oil was traded in the towns by local farmers, and some was used to make soap for export. It was said that wealthy Palestinians would even use olive oil in the mortar of their houses.

THE VILLAGES OF PALESTINE

'The Fellahin have a great love for their native place, and think it is a real hardship to have to settle elsewhere.'

CHARLES THOMAS WILSON[5]

Villagers gathering in the village of Halhul

There were over a thousand Arab villages in Palestine in the early twentieth century, and around thirty Zionist colonies. Two thirds of the population of Palestine lived in the countryside and farmed the land. The other third were the usual mix of professionals, tradesmen, merchants and government officials to be found in any long-established society.

Much information about nineteenth- and early twentieth-century Palestine was gathered by the Palestine Exploration Fund (PEF), founded in 1865 by a group of academics and clergymen to promote the study of biblical Palestine and the Levant. From 1871 to 1878 the PEF undertook a detailed and comprehensive survey of the topography, villages and towns, and archaeological sites of Palestine, led by two of its leading members, Claude Conder and Herbert Kitchener.

Their accounts of individual villages, buildings, topography and social structures paint a picture of a varied and self-sufficient society. These extracts are from a survey of the Tiberias area:

> *Ailbun – A stone village, well built, containing about 100 Christians. It is situated on a ridge, surrounded by brushwood, with arable land in the valleys. A good spring exists to the west of the village.*
>
> *Arrabet el Buttauf – A large stone built village, containing about 1,000 Moslems and Christians, and surrounded by groves of olives and arable land. Water is obtained from a large birkeh and cisterns. This was the place where Dhaher el'Amr's family was founded, and was long occupied by them.*
>
> *Deir Hanna – High walls all round the village, which is built of stone. The walls have round towers, and were built by Dhaher el'Amr's son, S'ad el 'Amr. It is situated on the top of a high ridge, and contains about 400 Christians. It is surrounded by olive-groves and arable land. Water is obtained from cisterns and an old paved birkeh to the north of the village.*
>
> *El Mansurah – A stone-built village, situated on the slope of the hill, containing about 150 Moslems; extensive olive-groves to south; water from spring and cisterns.*
>
> *El Mughar – Large stone-built village, containing about 1,100 Moslems, Druses and Christians, situated on the slope of the hill, with extensive olive-groves to the south and west; a large spring and birkeh gives a good supply of water.*
>
> *Yakuk – Stone built village, containing about 200 Moslems, surrounded by arable land, and situated at the foot of a hill; there is a good spring, and many cisterns are found in the village.*

In addition to a thousand or more villages, there were several large towns, each with their own character, determined partly by history and partly by social makeup.

Daily life in Hattin

Tiberias, on the Sea of Galilee. The 200-year-old mosque of Daher al-Omar is the large building on the right.

Tiberias was a 'mixed' town of Muslims, Jews and Christians, in northern Palestine on the shores of the Sea of Galilee. In the eighteenth century the town was the base for a powerful local sheikh, Daher al-Omar, who controlled most of northern Palestine. He built the mosque and citadel in Tiberias. For several decades during the eighteenth century, Daher was allowed to run northern Palestine as his own fiefdom, bringing economic prosperity, security and European trade to the whole area, and developing the urban centres of Tiberias, Acre, Nazareth, Safad and Deir Hanna.

JAFFA – THE BRIDE OF THE SEA

'The glory of Jaffa consists in its beautiful gardens, which stretch inland about a mile and a half, and extend north and south over a length of two miles. Oranges, lemons, palms, bananas, pomegranates and other fruits grow in thick groves surrounded by old cactus hedges ... '

C.R. CONDER[6]

In the early twentieth century the port of Jaffa was one of the most important cities on the East Mediterranean coast, and had a thriving economic and cultural life. It was the main port of Palestine from which oranges, soap, sesame and wine were exported. Besides the port there were soap factories and foundries in the city. The inhabitants established literary clubs, theatres and a cinema. It was in Jaffa that Issa Daoud al-Isa founded the popular newspaper *Falastin* in 1911.

The Arab town of Jaffa, used as a port of entry for many overseas visitors to Palestine.

Passengers and cargo were loaded and unloaded from ships moored outside the harbour using boats which had to be navigated through treacherous rocks by the skilled boatmen of Jaffa. One of the boatmen, Suleiman Girby, left an indelible impression on some of those visitors he helped from ship to shore:

> *Suleiman Girby, Arab Boatman, (Moslem) Jaffa. He was Head Boatman to Messrs. Thos. Cook & Son. He was a magnificent oarsman, & saved many lives, landing in rough seas at Jaffa, where the reef of rocks made winter landings very dangerous. Amongst those whom he saved were Pop. (sic) Blyth, & members of his family & Sir George Newnes, founder of The Publishing Co. & of the 'Strand Magazine'. Sir George sent him from England a gold watch, inscribed. The then Turkish Gov. of Jaffa coveted the watch, & asked Suleiman for it several times, and as he refused to give it the Pasha sent him to prison on a trumped up charge. As Suleiman still refused he was sent up to Jerusalem, to prison, where he literally pined for the sea; he was allowed out on daily parole, & spent many of his days at Bishop's House, and he gave this photograph to Miss Blyth. When the Pasha left Jaffa, Suleiman was sent back to Jaffa at once. He & his 2 brothers (only less good boatmen than he) died of cholera in the epidemic that swept Jaffa & Galilee (chiefly Cesarea & Tiberias) about 1905.*
>
> A HANDWRITTEN NOTE ON THE REVERSE OF A PORTRAIT PHOTO OF GIRBY

The Jaffa orange developed in the late nineteenth century by the Arab farmers of Palestine was noted for its quality. Most of the oranges shipped from Jaffa were sent to Liverpool for the British market.

A few Jews lived alongside the majority Arab population in Jaffa. Near the town there were also a number of Jewish communities; a German agricultural colony, Rishon LeZion, a Zionist colony supported by Baron Rothschild founded in 1882, and Mikveh Israel, an agricultural school set up by the Alliance Israelite Universelle,

Palestinian Arabs harvesting Jaffa oranges.

a French-Jewish organisation. The school aimed to improve the economic position of Jews in Palestine who were solely supported by overseas charitable donations. In 1907 Jewish immigrants set up a small European-style garden suburb near Jaffa called Tel Aviv.

The Alhambra Cinema in Jaffa

Nablus – City of Trade and Manufactures

'The town is surrounded with beautiful orchards and vegetable gardens ... Among these are to be found olives, figs, walnuts, apricots, mulberries, pomegranates, and vines with a few palms. Cactus hedges surround the gardens ... The bazaars are fairly good, and the place is the market for the wool and cotton of surrounding districts. The soap manufactories are also numerous.'[7]

In the eighteenth and nineteenth centuries Nablus was the centre of Palestine's trade and manufactures. The area was a fertile source of cotton, much of which was exported to Europe due to the interest and enterprise of the ruling Arab sheikh, Daher al-Omar. Later in the nineteenth century the town became famous for the soap produced there, made from olive oil brought in from the surrounding villages. Farmers would take the pressed olive oil into Nablus to trade, selling mainly to the soap factories. The town's market was a shopping centre for the local villagers.

The important trading city of Nablus

THE CITY OF HAIFA

'Haifa has gradually been increasing in importance of late years ... It has a market and bazaars, a Serai and mosque ... The Austrian Lloyd steamers touch here once a fortnight, and the place has a small trade.'

PALESTINE EXPLORATION FUND SURVEY OF WESTERN PALESTINE

The Mediterranean port city of Haifa had been growing in population and importance before the British came to Palestine. In the eighteenth century the coastal village had been expanded and fortified by Daher al-Omar. In 1905 the Ottoman government connected the town to the Hijaz railway used by pilgrims travelling to Mecca, and the town became an important port and transport centre for the region.

The port of Haifa seen from Mount Carmel

During the Mandate it was a major administrative centre for the Palestine government, and in 1933 a new expanded harbour was opened by the British. The refinery and terminal of the Iraqi Petroleum Company pipeline were established by 1939. By the end of the 1920s Haifa had also become an important centre for industry, with large Arab and Jewish companies trading in tobacco, cement, flour and oils.

From 1928 to 1939 the population of Haifa increased from 25,000 to 106,000. Many of these were Jews from Germany escaping persecution, and Arabs from the rural areas seeking work in the town.

JERUSALEM – AL QUDS

> *'This noble Jerusalem has been the object of desire of the kings of all nations.'*
>
> EVLIYA ÇELEBI, 'BOOK OF TRAVELS', 1671.

The city of Jerusalem has been coveted by every conqueror of Palestine. It has a crowded history and exerts an emotional power far beyond its temporal limits. For all the spiritual longing invested in the city, it is also a place where people lived, worked, and had to get on with each other on a daily basis.

> *'My family is probably the oldest family in Jerusalem. We have lived there since the Arab conquest, fourteen centuries ago, and in fact the first governor was from our family, and he gave us the keys of the Holy Sepulchre, which we still have. We have to open the church in the morning, and close it in the evening. I had my education at first in a Swedish kindergarten in Musrara quarter, near Mea Shaarim. And then at Rawda College, a national, private Arab college, which was an excellent institution. They had excellent teachers, they taught us Arab nationalism and Islamic teachings. This really imbued in me my national identity, to feel proud of ourselves, and it remained with me throughout my life.'*
>
> HAZEM NUSEIBEH

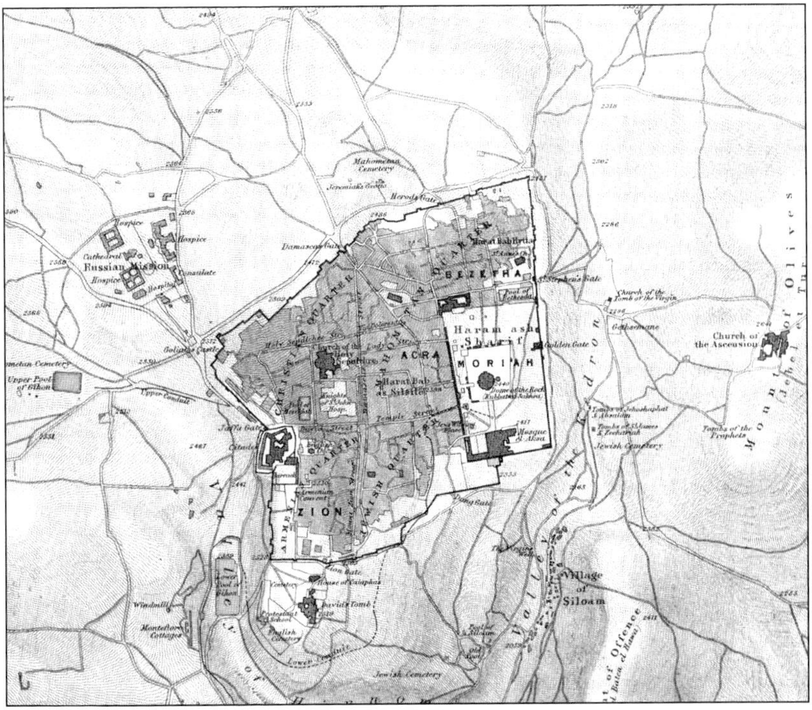

Jerusalem, about 1890. Little existed outside the walls of the Old City

Living areas in the Old City were divided into ancient quarters, reflecting well-defined communal divisions. In reality however, Jerusalem's Ottoman citizens shared living spaces, customs and friendships.

> *Musa (Alami) recalls that the child who became his own foster-brother was the son of the Jewish grocer down the street, and that for the next thirty years the two families used to visit each other, to exchange presents on each other's feast days, and to proffer congratulations or condolences as occasions demanded.*[8]

> *'We had a German Jewish maid, who looked after us in our childhood; she used to bathe us and so on. We had a Jewish plumber, by the name of Shabbatai; we had Jewish tenants*

in our properties. One of them opened a hospital in one of those very spacious homes; twenty-five rooms in Herod's Gate Quarter. On festivities my father would take us as children to a garment merchant by the name of Levi, in Bab al-Khalil in Mamilla Road and Jaffa Road, where he would buy us new suits and the two gentlemen would bargain in a very friendly way: – Oh, this is too much, two and a half pounds is enough for that suit. – Relationships between us and the Jewish community were then still normal, because we didn't understand what the Zionist designs were on Palestine.'

HAZEM NUSEIBEH

The Old City of Jerusalem seen from the air, some time in the 1930s.

At the start of the twentieth century Jerusalem's population was 41% Jewish and 59% Arab, (34% Muslim, 25% Christian). Some of the neighbourhoods of the Old City were mixed, others, nearer the main holy sites, were identified with the Muslim, Armenian, Christian and Jewish communities. New neighbourhoods were built by community leaders outside the old city walls in the late nineteenth and early twentieth centuries. These suburbs were more self-contained and socially restricted than the old quarters within the city walls. The Ashkenazi Jewish neighbourhood of Me'ah She'arim, for example, had its own synagogues and shops catering to the community.

Armenians had lived in Jerusalem from at least the fifth century AD. As Christians they came there on pilgrimage and some decided to stay. One of the four quarters of the Old City is the Armenian Quarter.

The Musrara Quarter, northwest of the Old City, was built by wealthy Muslim and Christian Arabs in the late nineteenth century.

The ancient city had an emotional impact on many of the British who visited Palestine.

> *It is rather a moving place – perched up in the barren hills of Judah that rise so abruptly out of the coastal plain, and seemingly such a strange place for the city which of all cities, with Rome and Athens, has influenced the world the most: no river, no fertile soil, just a barren stony mountain with olives and fig trees in the corries growing among the stones, kites and falcons overhead, and flocks of goats scrambling among the rocks... but the new city is much like any European town – more like a London suburb than anything else – with three streets of excellent shops and bristling with cinemas, dance-halls, synagogues, mosques, and every known type of Christian church from Coptic to Welsh Congregational!*
>
> Letter home, British Forces in Palestine, 26th July 1947

> *... the book shops in Jerusalem are wonderfully stocked with the latest books in English, German, Yiddish, Arabic, Polish, Rumanian and Russian – the tongues most common in these*

parts! However, everyone speaks English (literally – I have only met one Bedouin Arab and four Jews who didn't), and most Jews speak German or German-Yiddish fluently: how I wish I knew German.

Letter home, British Forces in Palestine,
24th August 1947

Gaza – Ancient City of Philistia

'Fine gardens surround Gaza ... There are many palms in these, and fine olive groves exist beyond them ... There is a bazaar in town, and soap is manufactured, as well as peculiar black pottery ... Cotton is sometimes grown, and dates, figs, olives, lentils, apricots and mulberries, melons and cucumbers are grown ... '[9]

Gaza is an ancient city, and has long been a trading centre. It was on the Arabian caravan route, and was a key location on routes between Egypt, Greater Syria and Arabia. Over the last 3,000 years it has seen the ebb and flow of the armies and occupiers of nation states from the Middle East and elsewhere, including the Pharaohs of Egypt, Philistines, Greeks, Romans and Ottomans. The ruins beneath its sands include Roman cities and Crusader cathedrals, and like other cities in Palestine it is home to people whose families have lived there for many generations.

'Palestine was a complete country; self-sufficient, prosperous, beautiful. One of the nicest countries in the world! I mean, it is no less than Italy, except that Italy is a larger country, but Palestine has the basic ingredients of beauty. You had the hilly regions; you had the plains; you had the Jordan Valley – Everything was beautiful, and plentiful, so I mean, of course it was a country. We go back to the Canaanites, we go back to ancient civilisation.'

Hazem Nuseibeh

Gaza city in prosperous times

2

Palestine and Europe

Europe Eyes the Middle East

For much of the nineteenth century the British supported the Ottoman Empire against threats to its territory, because they viewed it as a useful barrier to Russian maritime expansion. From the 1870s however, Britain, France, Russia, Austria and Italy began picking off selected pieces of Ottoman territory as the old Empire suffered military defeats. Britain's priority was to secure naval dominance in the Eastern Mediterranean to protect the land route to India, and later the Suez Canal, the vital artery of British imperial rule and global commerce.

In 1801 the British joined Ottoman forces to end the three year French occupation of Egypt. The British and French empires were in competition for the protection of their interests around the globe.

Ibrahim Pasha, ruler of Egypt, occupied Palestine and Syria in defiance of the Ottomans from 1831 to 1840. Britain and Austria helped the Ottomans to drive the Egyptians out of their territory by a naval bombardment of the Mediterranean coast. The allies called upon local people to rise up against the unpopular rule of Ibrahim Pasha, which they duly did.

In 1878 the Ottoman Empire agreed to transfer Cyprus to Britain, providing a naval base in the eastern Mediterranean. In 1882 Britain occupied Egypt, regarding the country, and the Suez Canal, as essential British possessions, vital to the maintenance of imperial communications.

A series of treaties during the nineteenth century between the Ottoman Empire and various European powers guaranteed extensive privileges and protections to foreign citizens in Ottoman territory. The European nations liberally awarded citizenship of their countries to people in the region in order to extend their influence. In early twentieth-century Jerusalem, for example, 25% of the inhabitants had foreign citizenship. This caused considerable resentment amongst local people as foreign consuls would intervene in Ottoman official processes to protect their citizens. Britain had a consul based in Jerusalem from 1838.

The challenge of the European powers to the Ottoman Empire was expressed in a wave of assertive building projects around the old city of Jerusalem from the mid-nineteenth century onwards. In 1860 the Russians built a large compound for the 20,000 pilgrims who

The German Emperor, Wilhelm II, entering Jerusalem under an arch erected by the Jewish community in Palestine.

came to Palestine every year from Russia. Italy, France, Germany and Britain followed suit and their churches, hospitals and schools loomed large on the Jerusalem skyline. The British built the Anglican cathedral of St George's in 1899. St George's School was attached to the Cathedral, attracting boys from Palestinian upper class families who were educated alongside British pupils.

The Ottoman government recognised that the European powers had designs on their territory. However, one of the Ottoman leaders, Enver Pasha, trusted and admired Germany. As Europe descended into war in 1914, Enver negotiated an alliance with the German government which he thought would protect the Ottoman Empire from the ambitions of Russia, Britain and France, known collectively as the Entente (French for 'understanding'). This resulted in the Ottoman Empire being drawn reluctantly into a war in which it had no interest and which would bring about the end of the 500-year rule of the Ottomans in the Middle East.

The Contradictory Promises of the First World War

With the Ottoman Empire drawn into the war, the Entente powers assumed that its defeat and dismemberment were inevitable. They negotiated between themselves which portions of the Empire they would take. The immediate priority, however, was to win the war, an aim which at times seemed far from achievable. The promises and agreements that Britain entered into during the war reflect an unhappy combination of their desperate need to gain an advantage over their enemies along with enhancing their imperial interests in the final outcome.

1914–16: The first promise – The Hussein–McMahon Correspondence

'Till now we have defended Islam in the person of the Turks; henceforward it shall be in that of the noble Arabs.'

Letter from British representative in Cairo to Emir Abdullah, 31st October 1914

In November 1914, when the Ottoman Empire declared war on the Entente powers in alliance with Germany, the Sultan also called on Muslims around the world to join in jihad against Britain, Russia and France. Millions of Muslims lived in the British and French colonies so this threat, although never realised, was a concern to the European powers.

By 1915 the war was going badly for the Entente; Ottoman forces were fighting back in Gallipoli, and on the Western Front there was stalemate. The British were keen to exploit any disaffection the Arab population had for their Ottoman rulers; they hoped that Arab and Turkish rebels and deserters could destabilise and weaken the Ottoman Empire.

Sherif Hussein of Mecca was appointed by the Ottoman Sultan as the chief religious authority over Islam's most sacred site. In September 1914 he was approached through his son Abdullah by the British High Commissioner in Cairo, Sir Henry McMahon, to sound out his loyalties to the Ottoman Empire, in the hope that he would help the Entente. In a correspondence that lasted until March 1916, McMahon offered British recognition and protection for an independent Arab kingdom, ruled by Hussein and his Hashemite dynasty, in return for the Hashemites leading a revolt against their Ottoman overlords. The negotiations over the proposed boundaries for this Arab kingdom were protracted and intricate; Hussein wanted specific commitments from Britain on boundaries, which the British were reluctant to give. Finally in a letter to Sherif Hussein from McMahon, dated 24th October 1915, a formula was suggested which both sides were able to accept. It included a form of wording which seemed to include Palestine in the territories that would be given their independence. The meaning of this formula would, after the war, be re-interpreted by the British.

In June 1916, the Hashemites began their revolt against the Ottomans. The Arab forces, led by Sherif Hussein's son, Emir Feisal, attacked government strongholds and the Hijaz railway. Captain T.E. Lawrence kept the Arab forces supplied with British finance and weapons. He was also an enthusiastic participant in the railway sabotage missions and the assault on the Red Sea port of Aqaba. In August 1918 this Arab Army joined General Edmund Allenby and his British forces in the taking of Damascus which ended the war in the Middle East.

1916: the second promise – the Sykes–Picot Agreement

As early as 1915, with bidding underway between Russia and France for portions of the Ottoman Empire, the British had to decide what their demands should be. The report of the De Bunsen Committee, commissioned by Prime Minister Herbert Asquith to consider this matter, was published in June 1915. The Committee recommended that Britain should maintain its influence in the Persian Gulf, and take control of Mesopotamia (Iraq). The port of Haifa in Palestine was identified as an important link in the chain of imperial communications with Mesopotamia, but the country as a whole was not considered to be worth coveting.

With these territorial aims in mind, British diplomat Sir Mark Sykes sat down with the French representative, François Georges-Picot, to negotiate a British-French agreement on the post-war division of the Ottoman territories in the Middle East. The agreement, concluded in October 1916, allocated zones of influence to each country, with Palestine designated as being under an 'international administration'.

1917: the third promise – The Balfour Declaration

> *'The object was to enlist the sympathies on the Allied side of influential Jews and Jewish organisations all over the world. It was hoped to counteract the efforts of the German Government to capture the sympathies of the Zionist movement, and to pave the way for effective propaganda in Russia and America.'*
>
> British Cabinet Paper, 17 Feb 1923.

When David Lloyd George replaced Herbert Asquith as Prime Minister in December 1916, Britain's ambitions in the Middle East increased, partly as a result of the long-term effects of Lloyd George's Biblical upbringing.

With the war at a critical stage, British efforts needed a boost; the War Cabinet wanted to keep Russia in the war on the Entente side, and bring America in as an ally. Arthur Balfour, the Foreign Secretary, had been approached by a group of British Zionists and persuaded that a statement of British support for Zionist aims would lead to significant advantages for Britain in the struggle with its enemies. The core of the Zionists' aims was the eventual establishment of an independent state for Jews around the world, along lines suggested by the Viennese writer Theodore Herzl. Dismayed by the anti-semitism he saw in Europe, Herzl published *The Jewish State* in 1896. In this book he argued a separate Jewish state was the only solution to anti-semitism. In 1897 Herzl convened the First Zionist Congress at Basel, Switzerland, and established the World Zionist Organisation. The aim of the WZO was 'to create for the Jewish people a home in Palestine secured by public law'. Herzl hoped to achieve this through negotiation with world leaders for a grant of land, in contrast to the small-scale practical efforts of Russian Jews who were establishing colonies in Palestine. He secured an offer from the British for land in East Africa but this split the Zionist movement, as many believed only Palestine could be the site of the Jewish homeland.

A key influence on the British government was Chaim Weizmann, a Russian Jew who came to Britain in 1904, aged thirty. As a chemistry professor at Manchester University he had discovered a process for producing ingredients for explosives which he offered to the British during the First World War at a time in which the need for munitions was at its height. This offer gained him access to senior figures already sympathetic to Zionism in the War Cabinet, contacts which he then used to lobby for British support for Zionist aims. Weizmann implied that Zionists had worldwide high-level influence, and that millions of pounds could be directed from Jews to invest in Palestine. This was based on the supposition that most Jews in the world supported Zionism; in fact only a minority of Jews supported its aims. Weizmann's eloquence captivated British Foreign Secretary Arthur Balfour, and the dynamic, biblically-inspired Lloyd George.

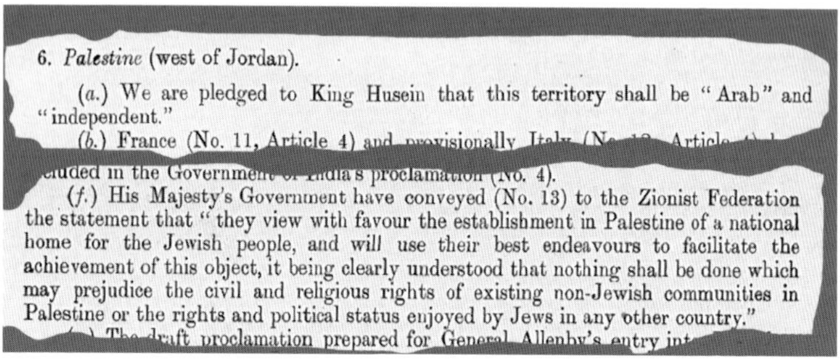

6. *Palestine* (west of Jordan).

(*a.*) We are pledged to King Husein that this territory shall be "Arab" and "independent."

(*b.*) France (No. 11, Article 4) and provisionally Italy (N...

...cluded in the Government of India's proclamation (No. 4).

(*f.*) His Majesty's Government have conveyed (No. 13) to the Zionist Federation the statement that "they view with favour the establishment in Palestine of a national home for the Jewish people, and will use their best endeavours to facilitate the achievement of this object, it being clearly understood that nothing shall be done which may prejudice the civil and religious rights of existing non-Jewish communities in Palestine or the rights and political status enjoyed by Jews in any other country."

... The draft proclamation prepared for General Allenby's entry int...

Two of Britain's contradictory promises spelled out in a single document, a secret Cabinet paper headed 'Memorandum respecting the Settlement of Turkey and the Arabian Peninsula', 21st November 1918 (CAB/24/72)

In September 1917, when Entente fortunes were at a low ebb – the battle of Passchendale was producing appalling casualty figures – Balfour took Cabinet time to argue that a show of support for Zionist aims would rally world Jewry to Britain's side. Russian Jews would help keep that country in the war, while American Jews would help bring their country in. He also pointed out, reflecting the thinking of the time, that Jews as a powerful, united force wielded a great deal of influence throughout the world.

Despite doubts and opposition from other Cabinet members and some leading members of Britain's Jewish community, a much-drafted letter to Jewish leaders declaring British support for Zionism, using wording drawn up with their active participation, was eventually published by the government on 9th November 1917.

Known as the 'Balfour Declaration', although at the time it had no official status and led to no formal government actions, Balfour's letter included the following words:

> *His Majesty's government view with favour the establishment in Palestine of a national home for the Jewish people, and will use their best endeavours to facilitate the achievement of this object, it being clearly understood that nothing shall be done*

which may prejudice the civil and religious rights of existing non-Jewish communities in Palestine, or the rights and political status enjoyed by Jews in any other country.

As the third of three mutually contradictory promises affecting the peoples of the Middle East in the war years, the Balfour Declaration embodied its own contradictions by implying that the rights of the current population of Palestine would not be prejudiced by the introduction of a national home for world Jewry into a country the size of Wales. It also introduced the phrase 'National Home for the Jewish people' into international politics, while failing to define what it meant.

The First World War in Palestine

'The locust invasion started seven days ago and covered the sky. Today it took the locust clouds two hours to pass over the city. God protect us from the three plagues: war, locusts and disease, for they are spreading throughout the country. Pity the poor.'

Ihsan Salih Turjman, diary 29th March 1915.

The people of Palestine suffered great hardship during the First World War. The British blockade of the coast caused severe food shortages, made worse by the Ottoman military impounding grain and the destruction of crops in a terrible plague of locusts in the summer of 1915. People died of starvation, or from cholera, typhus and other diseases.

To add to the prevailing mood of disaster amongst the people, Cemal Pasha, the Ottoman military governor of Greater Syria, which included Palestine, ordered a brutal clampdown on Arab nationalists or any other groups suspected of disloyalty. In 1915 a military tribunal condemned dozens of political activists to death in Beirut and Damascus, and hundreds of people were imprisoned or forced into exile.

Using a flame-thrower to control locusts in Palestine

During the War over 100,000 people died, were killed, or exiled. These catastrophes and the wartime brutality of Cemal Pasha turned many people in Palestine against the Ottoman Empire.

> *We more or less agreed that the days of the [Ottoman] state are numbered, and that its dismemberment is imminent. But what will be the fate of Palestine? We all saw two possibilities: independence or annexation to Egypt... Salute to the Hijazis. May God lead Hussein to victory, so that the blood of our martyrs in Beirut will not go in vain.*
>
> Ihsan Salih Turjman, diary 28th March 1915.

The people of the Ottoman Empire had long resented the privileges and protections enjoyed by foreigners under the Capitulations. Although these treaties stayed in place until after the war, the abolition of foreign postal services in the Ottoman Empire in 1914 was celebrated as the rejection of foreign influence.

As citizens of the Ottoman Empire, the young men of Palestine were subject to conscription. Recruits from the Arab areas of the Empire made up one third of the total Ottoman fighting force in 1914. Older men were conscripted into the labour gangs to build the services needed for war. This period saw improvements in communications throughout the Ottoman Empire, but at a terrible cost for the people who were forced to do the necessary work.

The British Enter Palestine

Ottoman forces tried to capture the Suez Canal in spring 1917. They were repulsed by British forces who then advanced to try and take Gaza, but the first two attempts were resisted by the Ottomans. Under the new command of General Allenby, British forces finally took Beersheba and Gaza in November. They then proceeded northwards through Jaffa and on to Jerusalem. The taking of Jerusalem was hailed as a symbolic victory for a Christian nation, but there were still many months of hard fighting before the Ottoman forces were driven out of Palestine in October 1918. This was the end of Ottoman rule in Palestine.

During the war, Britain had dropped propaganda leaflets from airplanes over the Middle East, including Palestine, encouraging the people to turn against Ottoman rule and offering British support for future Arab independence. The Anglo-French Declaration of November 1918 was issued to reassure Arabs then under British military occupation of the honourable intentions of Britain and France:

> *The aim of France and Great Britain in carrying on in the Near East the war let loose by Germany's ambitions is the complete and final liberation of the peoples so long oppressed by the*

The surrender of Jerusalem to the British, 9th December 1917, with the two sergeants to whom the city offered surrender.

> *Turks and the establishment of governments and administrations deriving their authority from the initiative and the free choice of the native populations.*

In view of following out this intention, France and Great Britain are agreed to encourage and help the establishment of native governments and administrations in Syria and Mesopotamia actually liberated by the allies, and in the territories they are now striving to liberate, and to recognize them as soon as effectively established.

Far from seeking to force upon the populations of these countries any particular institution, France and Great Britain have no other concern than to ensure by their support and their active assistance the normal working of the governments and institutions which the populations shall have freely adopted, so as to secure just impartiality for all, and also to facilitate the economic development of the country in arousing and encouraging local initiative by the diffusion of instruction, and to put an end to discords which have too long been taken advantage of by Turkish rule.

Such is the role that the two Allied Governments claim for themselves in the liberated territories.

Phrases like 'free choice', 'establishment of native governments', and not seeking to 'force on the native populations of these countries any particular institution' turned out to be irrelevant to the people of Palestine, as the picture of the post-War Middle East unfolded.

'The Balfour Declaration put Zionism on the political map. It was an alliance between British imperialism and Zionism which both sides gained from. The Balfour Declaration was a British ruse to take away Palestine from the French who got Syria – Palestine was part of Syria historically – and Palestine would have fallen to the Syrians without the Balfour Declaration. But the British needed Palestine to bring the oil from Mosul to Haifa. The British wanted Palestine for the pipeline, and of course to safeguard the Suez Canal, the way to India. And we [the Jews] provided them with a very good moral pretext for taking the country, and getting the country from the League of Nations, and it was an alliance, I think, to mutual benefit, except that the Zionists remained, and the British got out.'

URI AVNERY

3
The Division of the Spoils

The 1919 Peace Conference

'I am confident that the Powers will attach more importance to the bodies and souls of the Arabic-speaking peoples than to their own material interests.'

Emir Feisal, 'Territorial Claims of the Government of the Hejaz', 29th January 1919.

With the retreat of the Ottoman army from Syria in August 1918, British forces were left as the main military presence in the Middle East. In Palestine the British military command set up an administration of occupation, with its headquarters in Cairo. Worried about the effect the Balfour Declaration might have on the Palestinian Arab population, General Allenby's military administration insisted that it not be published in Palestine. In fact reports of the Declaration readily reached Palestine, where the Arab population organised meetings and petitions to protest at Britain's adoption of Zionism.

The victorious allies, principally Britain, France, America and Italy, met at the Peace Conference in Paris where they began to plan the post-war settlement with Germany and its allies, to suit their own needs. One element in this settlement was the question of Palestine, and the British, as a dominant partner in the Entente, were determined to promote the Balfour Declaration as the defining principle for the eventual governance of Palestine. The Palestinians sent representations to the British delegation attending the Peace Conference in Paris, but their ornately worded and politically naive efforts were no match for the special access given by the British to the Zionists, principally Chaim Weizmann, who was happy to tell representatives at the Conference in private what he meant by a Jewish National Home:

> *By a 'Jewish National Home' we meant the creation in Palestine of such conditions as should enable us to establish between 50,000 and 60,000 Jews per annum there, and to settle them on the land ... – that there should ultimately be such conditions that Palestine should be just as Jewish as America is American and England is English.*[10]

The Treaty of Versailles imposed harsh conditions on Germany and brought into being a new international organisation, the League of Nations. It was hoped that this body, advocated by United States President Woodrow Wilson, would resolve conflicts by negotiation and thus prevent wars in the future. The old-style annexation of territory by victors was rejected in favour of what was supposed to be a more enlightened form of colonialism, the system of Mandates, devised specifically for this purpose, by which victorious nations, 'Mandatories', would supervise those countries that were deemed not to be ready for independence. The League of Nations Covenant spelled this out:

> *Certain communities formerly belonging to the Turkish Empire have reached a stage of development where their existence as independent nations can be provisionally recognised subject to the rendering of administrative advice and assistance by a Mandatory until such time as they are able to stand alone. The wishes of these communities must be a principal consideration in the selection of the Mandatory.*
>
> Article 22, Covenant of the League of Nations, 1919.

While the victors were defining who could have independence and who wasn't ready for it, some of the people whose fate was being discussed took matters into their own hands. In March 1920 the General Syrian Congress, with representatives from Palestine, proclaimed Feisal king of an independent Greater Syria that included Palestine and Lebanon. For Feisal, this was merely acting on British wartime promises of Arab independence contained in the McMahon letters.

The King–Crane Commission

In May 1919 President Woodrow Wilson proposed to the Peace Conference that an investigative commission be sent to the Middle East to find out the 'wishes of these communities'. Britain and France, perhaps aware of what such a Commission might discover, declined to participate in the exercise. The Commission became a purely American affair, and Wilson appointed academic, Henry Churchill King, and businessman, Charles R. Crane, to lead the Commission.

From June 1919 the Commission spent six weeks travelling through Syria and Palestine, met with over 400 delegations, and received petitions signed by 91,000 people. The Commission submitted their report to the Americans in Paris in August 1919. In a summary of the evidence the Commission recommended that a united Arab kingdom should be established with Feisal as king under a temporary American mandate, and that as the majority of the people in Palestine were strongly opposed to the Zionist programme, the Balfour Declaration should be significantly modified. This inconvenient report was ignored by the powers determining the Mandates and quietly forgotten about in the United States after President Wilson's death.

Lloyd George Sorts it Out

> *'Mesopotamia ... yes ... oil ... irrigation ... we must have Mesopotamia; Palestine ... yes ... the Holy Land ... Zionism ... we must have Palestine; Syria ... h'm ... what is there in Syria? Let the French have that.'*
>
> The private musing of David Lloyd George, overheard by Intelligence expert Arnold Toynbee during the Peace Conference.

Once the idea of the Mandates system had been accepted by the major powers at the Peace Conference, Lloyd George, Prime Minister of Britain and Georges Clemenceau, Prime Minister of France, were left to decide between themselves how these Mandates would be distributed.

Lloyd George was determined to extend Britain's control in the Middle East beyond the confines of the Sykes-Picot agreement. He believed that Palestine was essential to the protection of the Suez Canal, and Haifa in northern Palestine was a valuable Mediterranean port. Control of Mosul in Mesopotamia would secure for Britain a vital supply of oil for its naval fleet.

The British grudgingly conceded Syria to France to gain Clemenceau's equally reluctant consent to British control of Palestine and Iraq. In February 1920 the two countries drew a boundary between Palestine and Syria. In April 1920, the conference of the Principal Allied Powers at San Remo endorsed the British-French distribution of the Mandates. British forces withdrew from Syria, and the French swept in to take control. Feisal and his embryo 'independent' government were ejected in July 1920, and his Arab kingdom came to an abrupt end.

Winston Churchill in Palestine, with T.E. Lawrence and Prince Abdullah

In March 1921 Colonial Secretary Winston Churchill, on the advice of T.E. Lawrence and Gertrude Bell, created the kingdom of Transjordan out of territory to the east of the Jordan River. Feisal's brother, Abdullah, was made king of Transjordan under supervision of the Palestine Mandate, and Feisal was compensated for his humiliation in Syria with the throne of Iraq vacated by Abdullah. Thus Britain secured a land route from Haifa to Baghdad, limited French ambitions in Syria, and gained two client kingdoms under the grateful Hashemites. Winston Churchill would even claim that he was honouring Britain's wartime commitments to Sherif Hussein. (Two years earlier, Churchill had written in a Cabinet memorandum of 'the Jews, whom we are pledged to introduce into Palestine and who take it for granted that the local population will be cleared out to suit their convenience.'[11])

Reactions in Palestine

In Palestine, the ejection of Feisal by the French from Syria was greeted with dismay by Arab nationalists. The Balfour Declaration, which was eventually publicised and discussed in the Arab press, created fear amongst the Arab population that the Zionists were about to take over the land. These fears were heightened by the ambitious demands of the Zionist Commission in Palestine and the public military training of Jewish immigrants by Zionist radical Vladimir Jabotinsky.

While, in public, British politicians denied that Palestine was to be turned into a home for Jews from all over the world, Balfour, at least, made clear to his United States counterpart what he saw as the country's eventual destiny:

> *We have got in Palestine to deal with a country in which the majority of the population are Arabs, in which there is an important Jewish minority to whom we desire largely to entrust the task of fitting the country, with the help of outside Jewish assistance, to be a home for the Jewish race.*[12]

British attempts to reassure the Palestinians were not helped when Chaim Weizmann and the Zionist Commission arrived in Jerusalem to act as liaison between the Jewish community in Palestine and the British military administration, and to prepare plans for the future development of the country. Allowed by the British to be the sole representatives of the Jews in matters relating to Palestine, the Zionist Organisation supplanted the traditional religious leaders of the diverse groups within the Jewish community.

The Zionist Commission might have seemed to Whitehall a good solution to the problems of administration in Palestine, but to the military government on the ground it was a headache, as one British administrator wrote in 1920.

> *I attach a list of the Zionist Commission's composition at their Headquarters and in the Districts. It will be seen that a complete administrative machine is operating, in fact its departments correspond in numbers exactly to my own.*
>
> *This Administration within an Administration renders good government impossible, the Jewish population look to their Administration and not to mine, and the Moslems and Christians can only see that privileges and liberties are allowed to the Jews which are denied to them.*[13]

In this atmosphere of tension, frustration and suspicion, violent rioting by Arabs occurred in Jerusalem in April 1920, in which five Jews and four Arabs were killed. Trouble flared up again in 1921 when Arab spectators became involved in a brawl between rival Jewish communist groups at Jaffa.

Unfortunately, the British had scaled down their troops, and the riots in 1920 and 1921 took them by surprise. Britain's repeated failure to ensure an adequate police and military presence in times of heightened tension in Palestine would have devastating consequences all through the Mandate.

In 1920 following the riots in Jerusalem, the Grand Mufti of Jerusalem, a religious leader and Palestinian nationalist called Haj

Amin al-Husseini, was exiled by the British for inciting the crowds. In July 1921, the High Commissioner in Palestine, Herbert Samuel, brought Husseini back from exile and appointed him Grand Mufti of Palestine and head of the Supreme Muslim Council. Samuel hoped that, as Grand Mufti, Husseini would keep the peace among the Arab population. In return the Mufti was given considerable powers over appointments and Islamic charitable funds.

The Grand Mufti, Haj Amin al-Husseini

BRITAIN'S INTERNATIONAL OBLIGATION

'You have got your start. It all depends on you.'

DAVID LLOYD GEORGE TO CHAIM WEIZMANN
AT THE SAN REMO CONFERENCE, APRIL 1920.

The terms of the Palestine Mandate were a triumph for Weizmann. It was his achievement to transform the non-binding British expressions of goodwill expressed in the Balfour Declaration into an internationally ratified constitution for Palestine, by incorporating the

Declaration into the League of Nations Mandate. British documents from this period show that Weizmann worked closely with Foreign Office officials in drafting the Mandate so that its terms corresponded with Zionists' demands. Weizmann continued to present himself as an international statesman, acting on behalf of world Jewry, and convinced the British there was a unity of interest between Zionism and Britain.

Prime Minister Lloyd George persuaded the Principal Allied powers (Britain, France, Italy and Japan) to accept the Balfour Declaration as a vital part of the Mandate for Palestine at San Remo in April 1920. 'Viewing with favour' the establishment of a Jewish 'National Home' had become an internationally sanctioned aim of the Palestine Mandate, even though there was no agreed definition of what the 'National Home' might be.

There are fifteen references to 'Jews' or 'Jewish' in the Mandate's wording, and none to 'Arabs', although they formed 90% of the population. There are three references to the Arabic language, in a clause specifying that Arabic should be used alongside Hebrew, on stamps and currency.

In 1922 there was a change of government in Britain, and the new Cabinet looked again at its commitments in Palestine. Despite reservations, they considered that Britain was honour-bound to keep to the terms of the Mandate, as a Cabinet paper explained: 'It is well-nigh impossible for any Government to extract itself without a substantial sacrifice of consistency and self-respect, if not of honour.'[14]

In July 1922 the British Colonial Secretary, Winston Churchill, issued a White Paper that sought to reassure the Arabs by claiming that Britain did not contemplate 'the disappearance or the subordination of the Arabic population, language or culture in Palestine'. But he declared that the Jews were in Palestine 'as of right and not on sufferance', and that Jewish immigration would be regulated by the number of jobs available in the country.

The House of Lords voted against the White Paper, but a few days later Churchill persuaded the House of Commons to reverse the vote. This was a blow to the Arabs in Palestine.

> *... the Executive Committee of the Fourth Arab Palestinian Congress declares today in the name of the Arab Palestinian nation which is determined to live in its land in self-respect, freedom and dignity, that it utterly rejects the resolution of the British House of Commons that is based on despotism and injustice, just as that House and the British cabinet have flagrantly violated the promises made by the British government in 1915 and 1918 to the Arabs of Palestine.*
>
> Statement by the Executive Committee of the Fourth Arab Palestinian Congress, 8th July 1922.

But at least, five years after the majority population was described only as the 'existing non-Jewish communities' in the Balfour Declaration, the British Government in their White Paper now acknowledged the presence of Arabs in Palestine.

4
The British in Palestine 1920–48

Government and Law

'... totalitarianism tempered by benevolence.'

Edward Keith-Roach[15]

Britain, as the Mandatory for Palestine, was supposed to be offering assistance and advice to the people of Palestine to prepare them for self-rule. Under the military administration set up during the War, the main task had been maintenance of the status quo, and in 1921 a new civil government took over, run from the Colonial Office, who were used to running colonies rather than operating the new-fangled Mandate system. The first High Commissioner, the Zionist Jew Herbert Samuel, had absolute power, working through an Executive Cabinet and Advisory Council, both composed of British officials.

Herbert Samuel (right), the first British High Commissioner in Palestine

The old Ottoman system of administration was largely swept away, and a whole raft of new procedures, based on British custom and practice, were introduced, including criminal and commercial law, town planning regulations, and land use and taxes. But the High Commissioner also introduced laws which were thought necessary for the particular needs of Palestine, including press censorship, trade tariffs and land sale regulations. This was typical of British colonial practice, which retained elements of the status quo but added new measures partly aimed at improving British control. Only in areas that had a particular cultural or religious significance, such as family law, were the old Ottoman statutes retained.

Civil servants

'Make your peasant happy and prosperous and agitation will cease.'

Humphrey Bowman, Director of Education in Palestine 1920–36.

The administration of Palestine was financed from the taxes paid by the people who lived there; the British government met only the costs of stationing troops in the country. The security and administration costs for Palestine were unusually high by British colonial standards. During the Mandate the number of government departments increased from twenty to forty, and the number of employees rose from 2,500 to 30,000. Ten per cent of these employees were British, usually the senior managers, and the rest were local people.

'I left school at fourteen, and went to work at a lawyer's office, I was a lawyer's clerk, and this lawyer was Jewish, an Oxonian. The whole office was full of crests of arms of Oxford colleges, things like this, and we talked English in the office, and some of our clients were British Mandate officers. My boss was the secretary of the Rotary Club for the British. The British accepted him as one of their own; they didn't consider him really a Jew, but an Englishman. So I had some contact, I saw the

people, I saw officers of the British Mandate, which was in a way funny, because by that time I was a member of the underground, fighting the British, and the British people I met in our office were generally very nice people. And so I was somewhat torn between my sentiments about it. Every Britisher at the time was a demi-god: they were the authorities, they were the government.'

Uri Avnery

During Herbert Samuel's period of office, hundreds of new classrooms were built, but owing to the small budget allocated to education, between 4% and 7% of the total, development faltered. The number of schools was insufficient for the Arab population, who had to set up their own schools or use the various missionary schools in Palestine. The Jewish community in Palestine set up many of their own schools, supported by donations from abroad. The Jewish Agency received a grant for education from the Palestine Government.

The Department of Health of the Palestine Government introduced compulsory inoculations against typhoid, cholera and smallpox. It focused on improving sanitation, measures against malaria such as swamp draining, and infant welfare. A particular concern was treatment for the eye diseases prevalent in Palestine, using mobile clinics. Only two hospitals were established by the Palestine government, one in Jerusalem and one in Haifa. People who could not reach these had to depend on the hospitals provided by missionary societies.

District Officers

'So deeply have we always been impressed by your love and devotion to our city and to ourselves, that we shall never forget it.'

Letter from two citizens of Safad to Sydney Moody,
District Officer for Safad and Ramleh, and official
in the Secretariat, 1924 to 1939.

The British ruled through their District Officers. Palestine was divided up into districts, and a British official was put in charge of the area. They were primarily responsible for tax collecting and security in their regions, overseeing public works and emergency measures such as dealing with floods or locust invasions.

Under the Mandate the British continued the Ottoman tradition of townspeople and villagers nominating mayors or *mukhtars* as community leaders. The *mukhtars* represented their community to the District Officer, and the District Officer would convey his expectations of the community's loyalty and subservience through the *mukhtar*.

Sydney Moody was a typical example of a District Officer. He served in Palestine during the First World War in the Royal Fusiliers. When the war ended he was appointed as a military governor under the Occupied Enemy Territory Administration, and in 1920 with the change to the civil administration he was posted to Safad as a Sub-District Governor. In 1923 he served a few months in Ramleh, and then in 1924 he was posted to the Secretariat in Jerusalem. By 1938 he had been promoted to Deputy Chief Secretary, and on three occasions he represented Britain to the Permanent Mandates Commission in Geneva. In 1939 he was posted to Mauritius as Colonial Secretary.

At the announcement he was leaving Palestine in 1939 Moody received a flood of letters from all sections of the Palestine community who genuinely felt his loss. The Jewish scholar I.A. Abbady wrote that Moody's service in the Galilee, '...is still looked back at by all sections of the Jewish population as their honeymoon with the British Administration', while *Falastin* newspaper of 1939 reported that with his departure, 'the Arabs will lose a sincere friend and an honest advocate'. His own summary of his time as a District Officer, sums up the complexity of the job:

> *'I spent 22 years in Palestine. I arrived there with Allenby's army at the third Battle of Gaza in 1917 and I left on Christmas Eve, 1939. But my father-in-law who was a distinguished missionary of the Church of Scotland in Palestine and had an intimate knowledge of every aspect of life in that country, once said to me: 'If you want to write a book about Palestine do it at the end of the first fortnight; because the longer you stay after that, the less you will feel you know about it.'*

The Palestine Police – the Thin British line

In the early days of British military rule, a police force had been put together from the remaining Ottoman officers. With the beginnings of the civil administration the Palestine Police Force came into existence, with procedures, uniforms, reporting systems and areas of authority. Senior officers were usually British, and Arabs and Jews were recruited into the ranks. The force was divided into two sections; the British Section and the Palestinian section, which included both Arabs and Jews.

In the tense and volatile atmosphere created by British policy, demonstrations and counter-demonstrations could soon escalate into riots and violence. The Palestine Police had the task of confronting and containing these protests. Although the Administration was keen to economise on security, the police force had to develop new structures, methods and equipment as episodes of violence taught grim lessons to the government and police command. The escalation of police defences reflected the deteriorating situation in Palestine.

After 1930, the separation that had existed between British and Palestinian police was reduced and the force became more integrated. British police joined the mounted patrols that had previously been undertaken only by Palestinians. Both sections worked together on routine police work.

There were many occasions in Palestine when police had to contain and control demonstrations. In October 1933, protests against British policy in Palestine were organised in the main towns by the Arab political parties. Building on previous experience the police equipped themselves with riot shields for the first time.

The Criminal Intelligence Department of the Police used occasions like the Jaffa demonstrations to gather information. They recorded the whole event in photographs, and developed techniques to estimate the numbers present. In Jaffa at the October protest the CID estimated the crowds at 7,000; there were fewer than 100 police officers.

When the demonstration deviated from the agreed route, the police held the people back and tried to disperse the crowd. They did this by repeated baton charges, mounted charges, and ultimately firing at the protestors. On the first mounted charge the police horses slipped on the street cobbles; after this incident horses were fitted with special shoes. In the Jaffa incident twenty-six demonstrators and one policeman were killed, and nearly 200 demonstrators and fifty-six police were injured.

From 1921 to 1926, there were two gendarmerie units which assisted the regular police in emergencies and patrolled the borders of Palestine. In 1926, to reduce costs, the gendarmerie units were disbanded, and the Transjordan Frontier Force was formed to take over the border duties.

1929 was a particularly tense year in Palestine, with feelings running high in Arab and Jewish communities in defence of the Muslim and Jewish holy sites in Jerusalem. British Constable Percy Drew describes having to confront an angry funeral procession for a Jewish boy who had been stabbed in a violent incident.

> *We prepared ourselves outside the Jaffa gate in Post Office Square with batons only. No shields but we did have steel helmets. When the procession arrived we could hear some Jewish leaders, or self appointed spokesmen, shouting in English as well as Hebrew to their supporters. They said such things as 'They are British and will not harm you.' They seemed to have no idea of the determination of our people although we were but a handful ... As they advanced they seemed equally determined to get through. I noticed lots of Arabs watching in silence, they seemed ready and anxious to join in if we lost control. Jim Munro was our senior officer present and I heard him say calmly 'Chin straps down.' Then after a moment he ordered 'Draw batons.' He then called upon the procession to obey the law and turn about, which they refused to do. It was very hot in the sun and we were sweltering and although grimly determined, most of us dreaded*

our job at that moment and wished we were somewhere else. We could see it was going to be a hell of a battle and I felt sick. Yet not one of us hesitated to obey an order, so we advanced and pressed into the crowd firmly but with considerable restraint. Not one officer used his baton at that stage, just gently pushing, like dealing with a London crowd. But scuffles developed in which a lot of us got hurt, so Munro then ordered a vigorous charge and led the way forward. I broke my baton on the very first head I ever hit in my life and was left defenceless. I found afterwards that this occurred to other officers too. But the mob was successfully restrained from entering the Old City that day.[16]

The Problem with the Mandate

'Self government by the Arabs must necessarily be based on a recognition by them of the obligation to establish the Jewish National Home. Until the Arabs recognised that obligation, Palestine must necessarily remain under the direct administration of the British government.'

Extract from Minutes of the League of Nations
Permanent Mandates Commission, 1930.

'No representative bodies that may be established will be permitted to interfere with measures (e.g. immigration, etc) designed to give effect to the principle of a National Home or to challenge this principle.'

Colonial Secretary Winston Churchill to
High Commissioner Herbert Samuel, 21st June 1921.

'What we ask is that this elected body should be truly representative of the people's wishes on all subjects connected to the country.'

Haj Tawfiq El Hammad, Palestinian Delegation to
Winston Churchill, Colonial Secretary,
London 22nd August 1921.[17]

Preparing the people of Palestine for self-government would have meant Britain recognising that the vast majority of the population was Arab and that any representative assembly would therefore reflect the majority views. But this was to admit the possibility that such an assembly could prevent the development of a Jewish National Home, seen by many Jews as a path towards Jewish rule of Palestine, and built into the Mandate at Britain's request.

> *The setting up of a Legislative Council in Palestine under present numerical conditions, cannot but react detrimentally upon the evolution of the Jewish National Home.*
>
> Memorandum on the proposed establishment of a Legislative Council in Palestine submitted by The Executive of the Jewish Agency for Palestine, October 1934.

In 1922 and 1928 the Arabs rejected British proposals for an elected legislative assembly because, if they took part, the government would require them to accept unconditionally the Balfour Declaration. In 1935 when the proposal was aired again it was the Zionists who objected, because they would not yet have had enough representation to have their own way in Palestine. Their supporters in the House of Lords defeated the proposal for a Legislative Council in February 1936. At least during the Ottoman period, Palestine sent MPs to Constantinople to represent the views of their people, but during the Mandate they had no formal democratic powers. Municipal elections did take place in Palestine, but the inhabitants of the country did not participate in national government.

> *'There was an eternal discussion, because there were the Arabs, there were the Jews, and the British government was in between. The Jews did not talk to the Arabs, the Arabs did not talk to the Jews, both sides talked to the British, and both sides had to bring up unending arguments to justify why they are right and the other side is wrong. So the Balfour Declaration*

> *played a very big role, not only that – the central street in Tel Aviv at that time was called – is still called – Balfour Street, next to Allenby Street, and King George Street, the three main streets at that time. We learnt in school about it.'*
>
> Uri Avnery

The sticking point in all attempts by the British government to carry out the self-governing requirements of the post-War settlement was the insertion of the Balfour Declaration into the League of Nations Mandate. Time and again, it was made clear to the British that the majority Arab population of Palestine would not willingly accept the transformation of their country into a Jewish National Home.

The best informed politicians about Palestine, such as Herbert Samuel, had come to understand that replacing the Arab population with Jews was neither just nor practical. In a debate in the House of Commons in November 1930, he said:

> *If there were any question that the 600,000 Arabs should be ousted from their homes in order to make room for a Jewish national home; if there were any question that they should be kept in political subordination to any other people: if there were any question that their Holy Places should be taken from them and transferred to other hands or other influences, then a policy would have been adopted which would have been utterly wrong. It would have been resented and resisted—rightly—by the Arab people. But it has never been contemplated.*
>
> *There are four reasons why such a policy would have been utterly impossible. In the first place—and this first reason alone would be amply sufficient—it would have been an unjust policy; and being unjust and contrary to all the principles on which the British Empire is based, it would never have had the approval of English public opinion and of this House, or the support of the Dominions. Secondly, it would*

> *have been impossible of enforcement. The Arabs are a high-spirited people, with proud traditions, and they would have had the sympathy and support of the whole Arab world, the whole Moslem world, in resisting any such policy. Thirdly, the League of Nations, which is the organ of the opinion of the civilised world, would not have endorsed a tyrannous policy of that kind. Fourthly, and lastly, any such anti-Arab, ruthless policy, would have reflected the gravest discredit on the whole Jewish movement, and a Jewish national home that was animated by a spirit of that kind would not have been worth having. ... The Jews have themselves suffered through centuries from oppression and it is inconceivable that they should have learned nothing from that oppression except how to inflict it, and that they should apply to others the injustices which they have abhorred in their own history.*

Samuel was both correct and wildly wrong in what he said. All the reasons as to why Britain *should not* turn Palestine into a Jewish National Home were valid. But all the arguments as to why they *wouldn't be able to* were very wide of the mark, as later events were to show.

5

Jews and Palestine

The Jewish National Home

'Palestine should be as Jewish as England is English.'

Chaim Weizmann, Paris Peace Conference, 1919.

Building on the deliberate ambiguity of the Balfour Declaration and the wording of the Mandate, Jews and the British were each able to argue for their own interpretation of the phrase 'Jewish National Home.' In 1935 a Zionist Executive Report described the Jewish National Home as 'a Jewish state on the way'. For Zionists, the Jewish National Home would be fully realised when Jews were the majority population in the country, and could form a national government. Uninterrupted Jewish immigration into Palestine was therefore essential.

'Every person in the world wants to live in a state of his own, where his language is spoken, where his culture is dominant, where he takes part in deciding what to do and how to live. To be master of his own fate. This is so basic and so natural that I sometimes wonder about people who don't understand it – many Israelis don't understand why the Palestinians want a state of their own. They just want it: everybody wants it. It's a basic human instinct.'

Uri Avnery

In preparation for the eventual Jewish state, Zionists in Palestine organised the Jewish community (*yishuv*) into a separate self-governing society with control of its own land, economy, education, welfare and political structures. The first elections for a community government had taken place in 1920, the same year that a secret Jewish militia, Hagana, was formed. From 1929 the Jewish Agency was the government of the Jews in Palestine; it raised taxes from the community to fund a civil service, and a foreign office with its headquarters in London.

'Economically, we had our own health service, our own school service, quite independent of the Mandate, and it was like a state within a state; a government within a government; there was a very strong national discipline – and very strong national institutions that could impose their will on anyone here because they were in complete control of the labour market, of the health system. You could not get anything if you did not follow orders.'

Uri Avnery

The Jewish Agency fostered loyalty to the National Home through secular, nationalist symbols: the Hebrew language, 'Hatikva', the national anthem, and the blue and white Zionist flag. The schools also taught allegiance to the Jewish National Home. Politically the Jewish Agency was dominated by a coalition of socialist groups under the leadership of David Ben Gurion, who had come to Palestine in 1905.

The Palestine government formally endorsed these developments in the Jewish Community Regulations of 1927, perhaps not realising that the majority of Jews in Palestine would become more loyal to the Jewish Agency than to their British rulers.

Both David Ben Gurion and Chaim Weizmann recognised that they needed British rule in Palestine to protect and facilitate the development of the National Home. Ben Gurion and other Jewish Agency leaders liaised with the Administration in Palestine, while Chaim Weizmann operated at an international level, rather like a diplomat for the Jewish National Home.

Creating a Hebrew Space

A strong element in the Zionist vision for Palestine was the idea of Jewish-owned land being worked by Jewish labour. The Jewish National Fund (JNF) was established in 1903 to purchase land from Arabs in Palestine with the stipulation that it remain in Jewish hands forever. The JNF supported settlers to establish farming communities and provided them with equipment. In the 1930s 130 new settlements were established in Palestine, and fifty-three kibbutzim.

Kibbutzim farming colonies fused the socialist and land-based ideologies of Zionism. They operated on collective and communal principles; all property was held in common and there was equality between all workers, male and female. Life on a kibbutz was very hard, and only a minority of Jewish immigrants lived there; 2.5% of the Jewish population by the end of the 1920s. The kibbutzim were ideal training grounds for the elite fighting force of the Hagana, and were the hiding places for significant quantities of smuggled arms.

During the whole Mandate period, Jews never approached a majority in Palestine. In 1920 Jews formed 10% of the population, in 1930 they formed 17%, even by 1945 they were only 30%. Most of the Jews who came to Palestine were driven there by the anti-semitism they experienced in eastern and central Europe, particularly in Germany after the Nazis came to power in 1933. Because of immigration restrictions in places like America and Britain, countries where many persecuted Jews would like to have gone, Palestine was one of the few places left. These people were not necessarily Zionists, but they were glad of the opportunity to start a new life in a place they saw as a refuge.

Although Zionist imagery promoted the Jewish National Home as a process of taking possession of the land through farming, in reality most of the Jewish immigrants who came to Palestine were urban professionals and business people, who preferred to settle in the towns. During the 1920s, about 100,000 Jews, mostly from eastern Europe, came to Palestine; eight out of ten of these settled in cities such as Haifa, Jerusalem, and Tel Aviv.

Tel Aviv was established by Jews as a European-style garden suburb of the Arab town of Jaffa in 1907. During the Mandate its population increased from 20,000 to 165,000 as immigrants settled there. By 1944 one third of the Jewish population of Palestine lived in Tel Aviv. In 1921, the British recognised Tel Aviv as an independent municipality, separate from Jaffa. Zionists were proud of Tel Aviv as a modern Jewish city, with a European culture. It was the centre of Jewish secular and political life.

'Ordinarily Jewish people in this country had no contact at all with Arab culture. There was a total separation between Jews and Arabs, including Tel Aviv-Jaffa, which were one city. I lived on the Jaffa side, which was very good, because the tax was much lower – but there was no contact at all between Tel Aviv and Jaffa. I would say that 99.9% of Tel Aviv at that time had not the slightest idea about Arabs at all; had no Arab acquaintances, certainly no Arab friends. Maybe in Haifa and Jerusalem, it was a little bit less so because Haifa was a mixed city, Haifa was always a rather good atmosphere between Jews and Arabs, comparatively, and in Jerusalem of course there were adjoining quarters, but generally there was no contact at all. You can safely say that 99% of Jewish Palestinians never had a real conversation with an Arab.'

URI AVNERY

For some Jews, the idea of trying to preserve a European identity in an Arab state was a mistake. The leading writer, Arthur Koestler, thought that if Jews were going to live in Palestine, an oriental country, they should try to assimilate:

> *The Jews made no effort to bring European culture to the Arab masses, nor to adapt themselves to those aspects of oriental life which would have enriched their own cultural pattern and at the same time made them appear less provocatively alien to the country. They did not learn from the Arabs to build cool and spacious houses which would fit the climate and landscape; they brought with them their architecture of the Polish small town and of German functionalism of the 'twenties. Their dress, food, manners and general way of life were transplanted like a prefabricated pattern from their lands of origin. Some of these were improvements in the country's way of life; others unfitting and in bad taste. There was no cultural symbiosis between the two races. The Jews came as conquerors.*[18]

Tel Aviv beach in the 1930s became a focal point for the Jewish inhabitants of the city to indulge in the western practice of sunbathing

New immigrant Yefim Gordin, from Vilna, gave his impression of Tel Aviv in a letter to his parents of 1929.

> *You can't at all imagine the frivolousness and impulsivity, the hedonism and empty-headedness that pervade in Tel Aviv. Jerusalem seems to me in comparison so serious, dignified and deliberate, and I like that.*[19]

JEWS AND ARABS COME FACE TO FACE

The British Mandate for Palestine created the ideal conditions for the development of group conflict amongst the people of the country. The terms of the Mandate identified a group, Jews from around the world, for special privileges, thereby creating fear and resentment amongst the majority population, the Arabs. The Mandate was supposed to be a temporary form of government, so Arabs and Jews knew they were in a race against time to establish the type of government they wanted. The British administration in Palestine did not have a vision of the country that they could work towards that would be consistent with the Mandate and fair to the population, so they allowed a situation to develop in which the people inevitably looked to their own communities for a vision of the future.

This uncertain situation fostered fear and suspicion between Arabs and Jews, and rumours of hostility by one side or the other, whether true or not, could ignite tension with catastrophic results. By undermanning the police force, the Palestine administration found itself unable to control the violence that broke out with deadly intensity in 1929.

Jewish nationalist agitation over Jewish rights of worship at the Western Wall in Jerusalem convinced the Muslim religious authorities at the Haram al-Sharif that the Zionists sought to demolish their holy sites on the Temple Mount and rebuild the Jewish Temple. Tension mounted as extremists on both sides made inflammatory speeches, and organised protests. When the violence broke out, hundreds of Jews and Arabs were killed in Jerusalem and all over Palestine as the Palestine Police and British troops struggled to restore order.

On 23rd August 1929, rumours spread that Jews were killing Arabs in Jerusalem. The rumours reached Hebron, with a population of 20,000 Arabs, and a Jewish community of 600–800 Sephardi Jews who had been there for 800 years. On the following day, an Arab mob from the surrounding districts came into the town, viciously attacked Jews and looted their homes. Sixty-seven Jews were killed, but 435 Jews were given refuge in twenty-eight Arab homes.

In the following days, violence broke out in other locations but it went largely uncontrolled because the Palestine Police Force had only 1,500 policemen in the whole country, and 175 British officers. Army reinforcements took five days to arrive. In the desperate situation, with massacres of Jews by Arabs in Hebron and Safad, and Jewish attacks in retaliation, the Police force recruited any British citizens who were in the country at the time, putting together a force from students, tourists and clergymen.

'[The Arab-Jewish divide] only came about after 1929, with the rebellion when the [Jews] intruded into the Haram el-Sharif area, the holy sanctuary, and people are extremely sensitive about the sanctity of these old places. So there was the rioting, and then the shootings and the massacre, and everything else. So that was the moment when there was this divide. We then said, well, those people are coming for something much more than simply augmenting their numbers. So there started the demonstrations, in Jerusalem, in 1933, and then in Jaffa, and all over the country, which climaxed in the Palestinian rebellion of 1936.'

Hazem Nuseibeh

British troops march through the streets of Jerusalem in a display of military force, August 1929.

Following these terrible events in October 1930 the British Government issued a new statement of policy on Palestine; the Passfield White Paper. The Paper stated that under the Mandate the British had an equal obligation to both Arabs and Jews in Palestine. Lord Passfield recommended limitations on land sales from Arabs to Jews, and on Jewish immigration to Palestine. This paper was criticised by Zionist supporters in parliament who feared the loss of the special treatment Jews had in Palestine. Chaim Weizmann and David Ben Gurion lobbied politicians, Weizmann in particular exploiting his friendship with Labour Prime Minister, Ramsay MacDonald. In a phone conversation between the two men, Weizmann virtually ordered MacDonald to disown his own government's White Paper.

> *[Lord Passfield] is causing trouble all the time. If a question is put to you in the House tomorrow, then you can still put matters right. If you will consult the Lord Advocate he will advise you as to the formula to be used. We have to deal with excited and anxious people and it is undesirable that there should be any misunderstanding... We are dealing with an administration in which we have no confidence, and in which I think you should not have any yourself.*[20]

MacDonald subsequently wrote a public letter to Weizmann which re-assured him that none of the Passfield recommendations would be implemented. The Arabs ruefully called this document the 'Black Letter'.

6

Arab Protest and the Arab Uprising 1933–39

The Background to Arab Opposition

'Awake! It is your homeland. Do not let it be sold to the strangers!'

Muhammad Is'af al-Nashashibi[21]

Arabs had been wary of Zionism from its beginnings. In 1898, the Cairo journal *Al Manar* had warned that Zionism aimed to take possession of Palestine. In 1908 the journal *Al-Karmil* was founded in Haifa to oppose Zionist colonisation. At least 600 anti-Zionist articles appeared in ten leading Arab newspapers between 1908 and 1914. The Balfour Declaration and the terms of the Mandate appeared to confirm the long-held fears of the Arabs.

Opposition to Zionism was political; to the Arabs its adoption by the British prevented the realisation of their hopes for self-government and independence. There was widespread fear amongst Arabs that under a Jewish state they would lose their livelihoods and their land, and that Palestine would become a place they did not recognise and in which they did not belong.

Arabs also complained of unfair treatment and discrimination under British rule: their not being given opportunities to bid for government contracts, trade controls that damaged their exports and protected Jewish commerce, lack of investment in education, and government spending on infrastructure projects, such as roads to Jewish settlements, that only benefited the Jewish population.

The British failed to take this fear and anger seriously; they believed that the benefits brought to Palestine by the combination of British rule and Zionist economic development would mollify the Arabs and reconcile them to the idea of the Jewish National Home. British aloofness and complacency only added to the Arabs' frustration.

By the late 1920s the traditional political leadership role of the established families was challenged by a younger generation of political activists, who believed in education, democratic representation and mass participation in politics. After 1929 many Arab political conventions took place, with young people and women getting involved.

A delegation of Arab women at the residence of the High Commissioner, protesting against the harsh treatment of Arab suspects following the August riots.

TIMELINE OF RESISTANCE

1932

'... the party feels that its greatest obligation is the shaping of public opinion and making it far-reaching among all classes of the people.'

MUHAMMAD IZZAT DARWAZEH, ISTIQLAL MEETING AT JAFFA, 26TH SEPTEMBER 1932.

The Istiqlal (Independence) Party was founded in 1932, one of several Arab political parties formed at this time. The leaders of the party were Mohammad Izzat Darwazeh, Awni Abd al-Hadi and Ajaj Nuwayhid; activists who had emerged from the professional and educator class rather than through the traditional family leadership. The Istiqlal Party proposed a strategy of non-cooperation with the British, through boycotts, demonstrations and press mobilization. They saw their opposition to British rule and the Jewish National Home policy as an anti-colonial struggle and they identified with the similar struggle in India. In their mobilization of the Arabs they were careful to avoid anti-Jewish rhetoric and prevented acts of anti-semitic violence at their rallies and demonstrations.

During the Arab rebellion of 1936 to 1939, blocking roads was one of the common tactics of the rebels. The police hastily had to clear the obstruction under covering fire from a Lewis gun mounted on the back of a truck. The man operating the Lewis gun was particularly exposed to sniper fire.

A police dog section was introduced by the British police in Palestine in 1935, using Doberman Pinscher dogs from South Africa.

1933

In 1933 Adolf Hitler and his anti-Semitic Nazi Party came to power in Germany. The persecution of German Jews that followed resulted in a sharp rise in the number of Jewish immigrants to Palestine. It now seemed to the Arabs that they were in a race against time to preserve their majority in Palestine. In October there were protest meetings, strikes and demonstrations in Jerusalem, Jaffa, Nablus and Haifa, against British support for the Jewish National Home. The demonstrations became pitched battles with the police which left thirty Arabs and one policeman dead.

1935

> *'The assembled declare on the 17th anniversary of the terrible disaster of British occupation of this land that the Arab cause is one of resistance and conflict between Arabs and the English who are responsible for all the disasters that have befallen the country ... Those assembled take the opportunity to hold the memory of the martyr Izz Al Din Al Qassam sacred ...'*
>
> Declaration by the National Meeting held in Jaffa on 9th December 1935 on the 17th Anniversary of the Creation of the British Mandate.[22]

Sheikh Izz-al-Din al-Qassam was a radical Muslim cleric in Haifa. He gained followers amongst poor and alienated young men there, and formed a military group that attacked British police and Jews. He was killed in a gun fight with British police in November 1935. He was revered as a martyr in Palestine and inspired others to take up arms.

1936

In April a six-month general strike was called by the Arab National Committee. Haj Amin al-Husseini, the Grand Mufti, had by now established himself as the leader of the Palestinian national movement, his period of co-operation with the British at an end.

> *As a sign of the dissatisfaction felt by the Arab nation in Palestine and in protest against the partiality shown by*

Government from time to time in order to strengthen the Jewish elements in this country and to annihilate the Arab national existence, it has been decided that a general strike shall be declared in this town as from tomorrow the 22 April, 1936, and we make the following demands to Your Excellency:

1. To stop Jewish immigration at once.

2. To pass legislation immediately to prevent the passing into other hands of the remaining Arab lands.

3. The formation of a National and Parliamentary Government.

Signed for the National Committee: Muhammed Ali Tamimi, Rashid Haj Ibrahim, Hanna Asfour.

Communiqué from the Haifa Branch of the National Committee to the High Commissioner, 21st April 1936.[23]

The armed resistance and the strike had widespread support throughout Palestine. In July 1936 Arab political leaders were arrested and interned in detention camps at Sarafand. The British authorities had built two camps, one for the middle classes and one for the fellah class. In a gesture of Arab unity the political leaders refused this division, and adopted traditional dress.

Arabs at Abu Ghosh taking the oath of allegiance to the Arab cause, 1936.

Fawzi al-Qawuqji, a Syrian nationalist who had led rebel forces against the French from 1925 to 1927, entered Palestine in August with 150 volunteers to join the rebellion. In October, the Arab states of Transjordan, Iraq and Saudi Arabia called on the rebels and the strikers to end the resistance. The leaders in Palestine complied with this request. Al-Qawuqji and his volunteers left Palestine and returned to Iraq.

During the Arab Uprising of 1936 to 1939, rebels attacked police stations, and some had to be evacuated. The British lost control of whole areas of Palestine. The government brought in Sir Charles Teggart, ex-Commissioner of Police in Calcutta, to advise on security. He ordered the building of around fifty new concrete forts, known as 'Teggarts' throughout Palestine, and a barbed wire fence running the length of the Palestine border with Syria and Lebanon to stop volunteers from other countries joining rebellions. The British spent two million pounds on this work, undertaken by the Zionist contract agency, Solel Boneh.

During this period of the rebellion, a thousand rebels and thirty-seven police were killed. The cessation of hostilities in October 1936 was to allow a British Royal Commission to visit Palestine, gather evidence and report on what should be done.

> *... we cannot – in Palestine as it is now – both concede the Arab claim of self-government and secure the establishment of the Jewish National Home ...*
>
> Royal Commission Report, 1937.

The Peel Commission Report included a recommendation that shocked the Arabs: Palestine should be partitioned into a Jewish and an Arab state. The Jewish Agency grudgingly accepted the proposal, especially as the report had spoken of 'population transfers', meaning Arabs being moved out of areas designated as Jewish. The Arabs rejected the proposal, and even the British government had to concede that the proposals could not be implemented.

Oh Palestine in your hills the last battle is existing between us and the tyrants, and for your dear independence the youths of your country are rushing into death in the face of mortar guns and shells.

Communiqué from Aref Abdul Razzak,
from the Office of the Great Arab Revolution
in Southern Syria, 2nd November 1938.

1937

In September Lewis Andrews, the district commissioner for Galilee, was assassinated by Arab rebels, and the revolt broke out again.

In October the British arrested 200 Palestinian nationalist leaders, deported many to the Seychelles, and outlawed the Arab National Committee. The Grand Mufti, Haj Amin al-Husseini, and Izzat Darwazeh both escaped the country before they could be arrested.

In November martial law was imposed, with the death penalty for the possession of arms. 112 Arabs were subsequently hanged.

1938

By October rebels had taken control of large parts of the country, and had captured the Old City of Jerusalem. The traditional Arab head-dress was adopted as a nationalist symbol by Arabs in the towns.

The situation at this time was such that Civil administration and control of the country was, to all practical purposes, non-existent.

Despatch on the Operations carried out by the
British Forces in Palestine and Transjordan,
1st August to 31st October 1938.

In November 1938, Major General Bernard Montgomery, the future Field Marshal, arrived in Palestine to lead the military fight against the rebels. He saw the rebellion as a war and expected a free hand in putting it down. 25,000 additional British troops and police were brought in to Palestine.

Regulations were introduced to ensure that certain villages were held responsible for the Haifa-Egypt railway line and each provided 'hostages' from its leading families to travel on the front of the pilot trolleys.

The rebels also mined the roads, killing soldiers in the trucks that drove over them. The army adopted a similar tactic to the 'mine-sweepers' used on the railways; a villager would be forced to sit on the bonnet of the lead truck in the convoy as a hostage. This was an early use of human shields in Palestine.

British troops rounded up thousands of Arab villagers and held them in detention camps. By 1939, the total number held reached over 9,000. The British army also carried out search operations on villages suspected of harbouring rebels or hiding weapons. Men and women would be separated and held in cages, sometimes for days on end. In the village of Halhoul near Hebron in May, 1939, ten men died after being kept in a cage for seven days without food or water. Women were made to bare their breasts to soldiers to prove that they were not rebels in disguise. Houses were roughly searched; and sometimes food stores were deliberately destroyed by soldiers. These searches tarnished the British army with accusations of brutality that remain in the Palestinian memory still.

> *We were greatly shocked to hear in the Press this week about the barbaric way a party of Jews were received by Black Guards at Sachsenhausen Concentration Camp. They were made to run the gauntlet between two lines of guards who beat them mercilessly.*
>
> *I was even more amazed to see a photograph last night sent home by a British soldier showing an Arab apparently running the gauntlet between two lines of British soldiers who were using big sticks and the butts of rifles... The soldier who sent it had written on the back 'This is how we made the "Wog" talk. Wouldn't the Berlin boys make a shout about this if they saw it?' One British soldier has his stick up in the air and the Arab is jumping to escape the blow.*
>
> Letter from Miss Rathbone to Mr McDonald,
> 30th November 1938[24]

Parties of troops move along street by street and house by house. Each house as they reach it is cleared of its male inhabitants, who are passed by military patrols to a large collecting centre usually located in an open square or space. Here the inhabitants are required to squat or sit on the pavement. A little drill is at this stage frequently imparted. The troops explain through an interpreter that any man standing up without a previous command to do so will be shot. The command is then given in English 'Up' – then 'Down' – Up, Down, and then a quicker tempo 'Up-Down-Up-Down'. Anyone not quick enough gets a kick up the backside. Due subjection having been thus established en masse, the male populace is interrogated man by man. 'Where do you live? What is your work?' etc. This goes on till dusk, when the balance still uninterrogated are marched off to a prison camp until the morning.

Letter from British resident in Palestine, commenting on War Office statement defending British soldiers against accusations of brutality.[25]

British intelligence officer Orde Wingate set up special night squads that visited random punishments on villagers with lootings, beatings, torture humiliations and killings. The Jewish Agency helped to fund the night squads, and Jewish settlers would join the forays.

Perhaps the most dramatic of all was the night action at Kafr Lidd, in the centre of the historic Plain of Esdraelon, where five special Night Squads surrounded a gang resting in the village, killing fourteen and capturing two, together with some important documents.

Despatch on the Operations carried out by the British Forces in Palestine and Transjordan, 1st August to 31st October 1938.

From 1936, the British army had imposed collective punishments upon villages or towns near scenes of rebel activity. In 1938 and 1939 this practice continued, and an estimated 2,000 houses were destroyed between 1936 and 1940.

Villagers in Lydda help to salvage the owner's belongings from a house blown up on British military orders, 1936.

By June 1939, the rebellion had been effectively crushed by the British. Many British soldiers, British police and 5,000 Arabs had been killed during the Uprising. The political leadership and the military capacity of the Arabs in Palestine were significantly diminished by this episode.

'In 1936, the silence of Jerusalem at night was broken by a few rifle shots which were not aimed at any place, but they signalled the start of the Palestinian rebellion of 1936. There was the strike of six months, and then it turned into an armed rebellion. At first it started honourably, and everybody

supported it, but unfortunately in '36 it degenerated into feuds. You know, Palestinians unfortunately are in the habit of getting into feuds. So that spoiled the whole thing. But still it was a concerted, persistent, successful effort, which made the British government decide to recognise Palestinian independence – the White Paper – and they said that this would be implemented in ten years, because World War Two was coming and they could not, of course, abandon Palestine immediately.'

Hazem Nuseibeh

7
Zionists against Britain

Britain Attempts to Resolve the Crisis

'The Board of Deputies declared its uncompromising opposition to any solution of the problem of Palestine which would impose on the Jewish people the status of a permanent minority in that country.'

Resolution on Palestine adopted by the Board of Deputies of British Jews, 16th January 1938

In 1939 with a full-blown rebellion in Palestine and war looming, Britain had to assert control over Palestine to realise its value as a strategic territorial asset. A formula for peace was urgently required.

The British government organised a conference in London in February 1939 to which Arab and Zionist leaders were invited. This was the first time that Arabs from Palestine had been allowed to participate in discussions about the future of their country. As the essential argument between the Arabs and the Zionists was over which group would govern in Palestine after the British left, there was no possibility of an agreement.

The British imposed their own policy on Palestine in the White Paper of May 1939. By this new policy, Jewish immigration to Palestine was limited to 75,000 people over five years. After that, Arab consent would be required for further immigration. This figure would maintain the Jewish population at 35% of the total. Land purchases in Palestine by Jews were restricted to certain areas. Finally the paper promised that after ten years an independent government would be formed composed of Arabs and Jews, with safeguards to protect the interests of both communities.

I managed to get a copy of the 1939 White Paper in English the night before it was published. I read it more than once and I could not believe my eyes. I would not have believed that England, whose policies (and politicians' positions) on Palestine I have observed closely, would be as fair to the Arabs as they were in this White Paper ...

AHMAD SAMIH KHALIDI (1896–1951),
EDUCATOR, WRITER AND SOCIAL REFORMER,
AND HEAD OF THE ARAB COLLEGE FROM 1925 TO 1948.[26]

'Unfortunately the Palestinian leadership were not up to the task, really. If they were, perhaps we might have mitigated the disaster which befell. So they rejected the White Paper, even though it recognised the Palestinian case. They rejected it on grounds that it should be immediate as a culmination of the rebellion, and not after ten years. And the British told them, 'but we cannot give you independence now, because we are in a life and death struggle' which was the fact.'

HAZEM NUSEIBEH

As the war approached Britain had to consider its position in the Middle East. Given the appalling treatment of Jews in Germany, Britain knew they could rely on Jewish support, but they could not be so sure of Arab loyalty and submission to British rule.

THE ZIONISTS AND THE WHITE PAPER

'The Commander states the Irgun Zvai Leumi means "national military organization". It was organised some ten years ago. Its object is to bring about the liberation of the country from the foreign yoke, the attainment of freedom for the Jewish people and the restoration of Jewish rule in Eretz Israel.'

REPORT OF CONFERENCE BETWEEN REPRESENTATIVES
OF THE UNITED NATIONS SPECIAL COMMITTEE FOR
PALESTINE AND REPRESENTATIVES OF THE IRGUN ZVAI LEUMI,
24TH JUNE 1947

Loyalty meeting in Hebron over cups of tea, with the Mufti of Hebron and local dignitaries, and British administrator, Edward Keith-Roach.

David Ben Gurion, the leader of the Jewish Agency, took a pragmatic attitude to the White Paper. 'We shall fight the War as if there was no White Paper,' he said, 'and the White Paper, as if there was no War.' He realised that in the crisis of war he would have to bide his time before openly challenging British policy. Right-wing Zionists however, accused the British government of abandoning the Balfour Declaration; they could not accept restrictions on immigration and land purchase in the country they already regarded as theirs.

The Irgun Zvai Leumi had formed in response to Arab attacks on Jews during the 1936–39 Uprising. From 1937 to May 1948 over 400 Arabs were killed by Irgun acts of terrorism.

'I joined the Irgun around my 15th birthday, that was at the end of 1938, and I was there for some years, and I left Irgun later on – which was very unusual. But for those years, quite formative years of my life, I was an honest-to-goodness member of a terrorist organisation. To me it was simple and straightforward: this is our country, the British have nothing to do here, so let's kick them out.

Aftermath of the King David Hotel bombing.

I joined immediately after the British hanged the first Jewish Underground member, which was in the autumn of 1938. His name was Shlomo Ben Yusuf, and he was caught after firing (ineffectually, I must say) on an Arab bus near Safad. He was sentenced to death, and he was actually hanged. This got me so excited that I decided to join immediately.

I left the Irgun in 1942. I got more and more disaffected with the Irgun ideology, the Irgun political group line, with their attitude towards the Socialist movement, the Workers' movement, their attitude towards the Arabs, and I did not believe any more in terrorism.'

URI AVNERY

From 1944, militant Zionist groups adopted terrorist tactics against the British in Palestine, targeting the police, the military, communications and offices of the Administration. By 1945 it was clear to Ben Gurion that the new Labour government in Britain had retreated from its support for a Jewish state. He therefore agreed that the authorized Hagana could join forces secretly with illegal terrorist groups, including Irgun, LEHI, and the Stern Gang in attacks on government property in Palestine, even collaborating on the devastating attack on the King David Hotel in July 1946, which killed ninety-one people, mainly civilian workers for the British administration.

After this, Ben Gurion decided that the priority was to maintain relations with the British while the Jewish Agency prepared for the war with the Arabs they saw as inevitable.

THE REFUGEE SHIPS

When the British imposed limitations on Jewish immigration in the 1939 White Paper, Zionist organisations in Europe and Palestine arranged for refugees to be illegally brought in by land and sea. Some smaller ships with a few hundred passengers landed at night and the refugees were spirited away to Jewish settlements, with British police and soldiers at times turning a blind eye to their arrival.

The 1939 White Paper immigration quota of 75,000 had been fulfilled in 1944, but the British allowed Jewish immigration to continue at 18,000 people a year. Once the war was over, the Jewish Agency launched a public campaign to transfer refugees living in Displaced Persons camps in Europe to Palestine. Between 1939 and 1947 sixty ships brought in about 20,000 illegal Jewish immigrants from Europe.

The ships were barely seaworthy, overcrowded and insanitary. They openly challenged the British naval blockade of the Palestine coast in dramatic confrontations that were widely reported around the world. British policy in Palestine was condemned as heartless, and British prestige was damaged.

If they were caught when they landed, the immigrants were transferred to other ships by British soldiers and sailors, to be transported to Cyprus, or Mauritius. There they were supported by the Palestine Government, and gradually allowed into Palestine. Of the 18,000 Jewish immigrants in 1946, more than half were unauthorized. By 1st April 1947, there were 11,900 Jews in the Cyprus detention camp, waiting to enter Palestine.

The most notorious of the refugee ships was the *Exodus*, with 4,500 Jewish Holocaust survivors on board, which had been organised by the Hagana. When it arrived in Haifa the passengers were refused entry by the British and were shipped back to Europe, where they ended up in a refugee camp in Germany. This controversial episode further damaged Britain's international reputation, and took place in front of the watchful presence of the United Nations Special Commission on Palestine.

The British Front Line

To cope with the crisis in Palestine, from 1944 the ranks of Palestine Police were expanded by British recruits on national service. When the war ended Imperial Reserve troops stationed in Palestine were called upon to assist the police. In combined operations, the police and the military would search Jewish settlements and undertake large scale screen and search operations in the major towns.

By the end of 1946, Britain had 16,000 British and local police and more than 100,000 British troops stationed in Palestine. There was one soldier or policeman for every eighteen persons. The High Commissioner had the power to enforce martial law, press censorship and collective fines, although under intense and often hostile foreign press coverage and pressure from Zionist sympathisers in the British Parliament these measures were never fully applied. The Arabs were angered and mystified that the harsh treatment they received during their 1936–39 uprising was not applied to the Jewish community.

In February 1947, in Operation Polly, the families of British administrators were evacuated from Palestine. The remaining Britons were guarded in wire-enclosed security zones. The Government of Palestine's estrangement from its citizens was complete.

8

Britain's Crisis in Palestine

The Crisis of the Mandate

'On the strength of our word the Jews have come to Palestine and established their national home there: it would surely be one of the greatest betrayals in history to abandon them now to their fate as a minority in an independent Arab state. Nor is it to be expected that the Jews, whose strength is already one third in population and predominant in wealth, will ever agree to subordinate their progressive modern "European" community to the domination of a relatively backward Arab majority whom (in some respects justly) they despise.'

Colonial Office official J.M. Martin, January 1947.[27]

By 1946, the terms of the Mandate had created a crisis for Britain's control of Palestine. By supporting the Jewish National Home in the Balfour Declaration and the Mandate, the British gave public encouragement to Zionist ambitions. They thus offended the Arabs by ignoring their political aspirations and majority status in Palestine, and spread fear amongst them of their dispossession under future Jewish dominance. British politicians assumed they could manage this situation, and had not anticipated the strength of opposition from Arabs, and later from Jews, to their shifting policies.

Arab and Jewish leaders did meet to try and find a formula that would be acceptable to both, but neither was prepared to accept being governed by the other in Palestine. The Arabs were the majority of the population, and they had lived there for over a thousand years. Most of the Jewish population had no long-term connection with the land. But the Zionists would not abandon their goal of statehood, for which they had worked since 1917 with British encouragement.

The British government made one final effort to find an agreement acceptable to all parties at a conference in London which lasted from September 1946 to January 1947, but this too failed. By February 1947 the government was facing severe criticism from the British press and the public over the sacrifice of British lives and resources in Palestine. Britain decided to take the problem of Palestine to the United Nations, the inheritor of the mandates system, to see if they could come up with a solution.

THE INTERNATIONAL DIMENSION

'Clem, about Palestine. According to the lads in the Office, we've got it wrong. We've got to think again.'

ERNEST BEVIN, FOREIGN SECRETARY, TO CLEMENT ATTLEE, LABOUR PRIME MINISTER, 1945.

A new British Labour government was elected in July 1945. Before gaining power, the Labour Party had supported the Jewish National Home policy in Palestine, and had even spoken of moving Arabs out of the country.

On gaining office, however, Foreign Secretary Ernest Bevin had to look beyond party politics and consider Britain's national interests. According to his diplomatic and military advisers Palestine was a vital base in the Middle East, and a buffer zone to protect Suez. Bevin therefore needed to maintain British control of Palestine, and good relations with the other Arab states in the region. He decided in the short term to maintain the measures of the 1939 White Paper, whilst trying to come up with a permanent solution for Palestine.

After the Second World War, Britain was heavily in debt and needed a loan from the United States. Britain and America were also attempting to remedy the chaotic situation in Europe where there were millions of homeless and stateless people. Bevin realised that Britain would need the military and political support of the United States to maintain order and control in Palestine.

In 1942, Chaim Weizmann had won support from American Jews for the immediate creation of a Jewish commonwealth in Palestine. After the war Zionist Jews persuaded President Truman that allowing the stateless Jews of Europe into Palestine would help the European refugee problem and was a moral obligation owed to the Jews after their sufferings during the war. Truman angered the British by publicly demanding the immediate entry of 100,000 Jewish refugees into Palestine.

America did not offer any military help against Zionist acts of terror in Palestine. Moreover, the United States Congress opposed any relaxation of America's own strict immigration laws, which would have greatly eased the refugee problem in Europe and the pressure upon Palestine. Despite their co-operation in examining the problems in Palestine through the Anglo-American Committee of 1946, the United States did not provide any practical help to Britain, nor, for that matter, to the Jews in Palestine.

The Anglo-American Inquiry of 1946 was one of many official groups which visited Palestine in search of a solution. Like many before it, it failed to offer any proposals acceptable to all parties.

After the Second World War the strategic arrangements upon which Britain had based its Middle East policy for over twenty years were unravelling. The mandate for Iraq had ended with that country's independence in 1932, Transjordan was moving towards independence, achieved in 1946, and in Egypt the British were encountering resistance to their proposals for a military presence. This left Palestine as Britain's last foothold in the region.

Although the decision to quit India was made in 1947, Britain was still keen to hold on to Palestine. Britain, fearing Soviet expansion towards the Mediterranean, wanted to maintain control of the Haifa oil terminal and port. After 1945 the British government hoped to find a solution to the Palestine problem that included Britain retaining control of military bases in the country.

The Politics of Partition

'We are not going to the United Nations to surrender the Mandate. We are ...setting out the problem and asking for their advice as to how the Mandate can be administered. If the Mandate cannot be administered in its present form we are asking how it can be amended.'

British Colonial Secretary Arthur Creech Jones,
March 1947.

The United Nations appointed an eleven-nation committee in April 1947 to consider the Palestine problem, and report back by September. The United Nations Special Committee on Palestine (UNSCOP) spent five weeks in Palestine, toured the country and heard representations in special hearings.

'Then there came the United Nations commission. I remember one of the great events of my life: we had a yearly folk-dancing festival in the open, somewhere in the Carmel mountains, in a kind of big natural amphitheatre. And folk-dancing at that time was very central to the Hebrew culture, and there all the

young people went. There must have been 20, 30, 40 thousand people in this amphitheatre, and in the middle of it, it was announced that members of the United Nations Commission were coming to visit. So the whole thirty or forty thousand people stood on their feet and started to sing the national anthem with such an expression - such excitement, it was a very, very moving moment.'

URI AVNERY

In September UNSCOP produced a report which recommended the division (partition) of Palestine into two states, one Jewish, one Arab, and conferring international status on the city of Jerusalem.

Now the United Nations General Assembly had to vote on the recommendations and the weeks leading up to the vote were fraught with lobbying from both sides, with the Jews campaigning for partition, which would give them some of Palestine, but with a large Arab population, while the Arabs campaigned against being deprived of a large area of their country and population.

'The United States Delegation are now undoubtedly putting pressure on other Delegations to support partition and are trying to rush matters to a final vote with as little discussion as possible.'

FROM BRITISH DELEGATION TO UNITED NATIONS
TO THE FOREIGN OFFICE, 24TH NOVEMBER 1947.

The final vote was very close, but a combination of bribes and threats by Zionists and other supporters of Partition led to several nations changing their votes in order to favour the resolution to hand over a large area of Palestine for a Jewish state.

In November 1947 the United Nations General Assembly at New York voted to support this recommendation. If four nations had voted differently, the resolution would not have been passed.

'In 1947, when partition was adopted by the General Assembly of the United Nations, we were all dismayed, we were shocked, because Palestine was a unified territory, and we were faced with a situation where we were told it was going to be vivisected, partitioned. So there was rioting in Jerusalem, and elsewhere which could have been contained, it was spontaneous, but apparently the Jews were intent on getting us into that fight, because they knew that we were totally unprepared. The entire population of Jerusalem did not have a rifle. None. So I remember, after these three days of rioting they started bombarding our quarters and Sheikh Jarrah quarter. They got us into the war. There was not one single meeting of the Arab High Committee to say what we should do.'

HAZEM NUSEIBEH

The British announced in September that the Mandate for Palestine would end on 14th May 1948, and they would leave the country. They made it clear to the United Nations that they would not implement the partition recommendation, nor would they allow any delegations for the United Nations into Palestine until the beginning of May 1948. After the November vote, delegates at the United Nations discussed how to implement the partition proposal, but failed to come up with a plan.

By February 1948, the United Nations still had no plan for enforcing partition, and the United States proposed that the partition plan be abandoned as impracticable and a trusteeship for Palestine be implemented instead. The Mandate came to an end while this was still being discussed.

'I remember, when the British declared that they were going to leave the country, I don't think we really believed them, we thought that the perfidious British were perfidious like always, were really creating a bluff. But slowly we became used to the idea.'

URI AVNERY

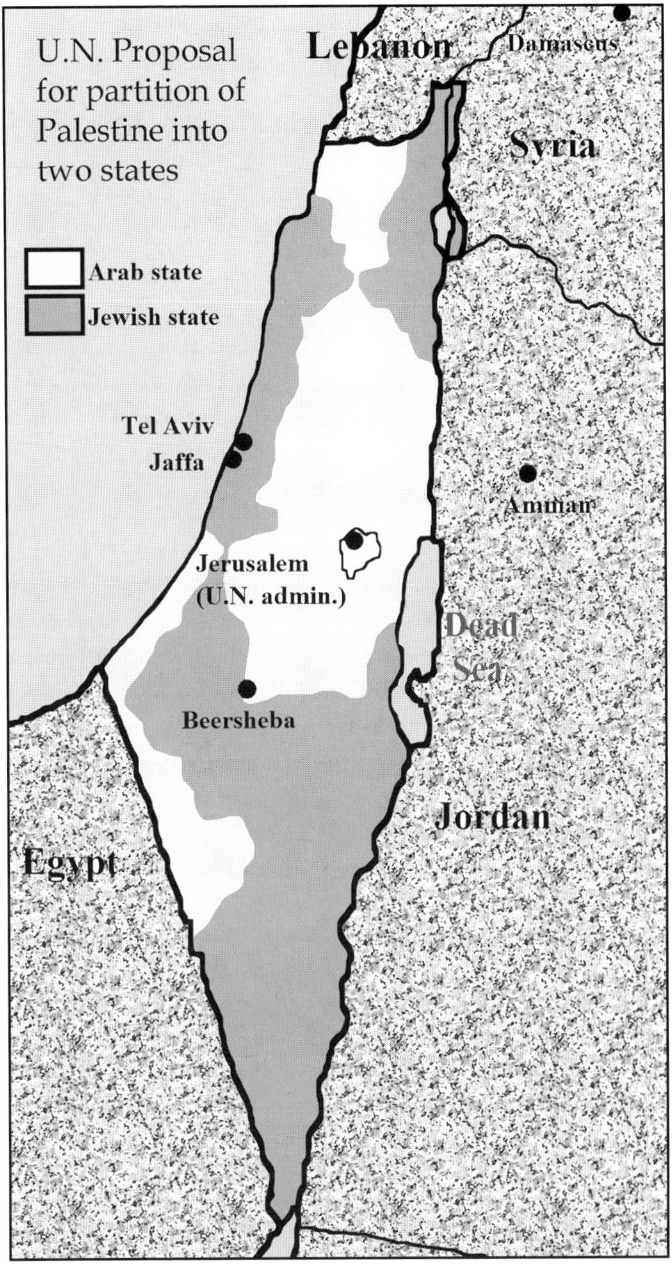
U.N. Proposal
for partition of
Palestine into
two states
Arab state
Jewish state
Lebanon
Damascus
Syria
Tel Aviv
Jaffa
Amman
Jerusalem
(U.N. admin.)
Dead
Sea
Beersheba
Jordan
Egypt

'When the British High Commission gave an address to the people of Palestine, he said that the British government and administration and army will be withdrawing from Palestine within six months and he fixed the day on the 15th May 1948, and when the word spread I remember talking to my uncle and he said 'Do you believe what he said? The British would leave London before they withdraw from Jerusalem.' In other words many people were incredulous that the British would actually abandon Palestine.

We had not yet absorbed the total dimensions of the story. After all, we lived in an established situation, Palestine was there, Jerusalem was there, we were the vast majority of the country so it was the status quo, it would take people of great imagination to think of an alternative.'

HAZEM NUSEIBEH

The contortions of the boundaries in the United Nations Partition proposal illustrate the problems of trying to allocate territory exclusively to particular groups. Although Jews comprised just one third of the total population and owned only six per cent of the land, fifty-five per cent of Palestine was assigned to their state. A large number of Arabs lived in areas that would come under Jewish control; they would have comprised one third of the population. From the 1930s Zionists had realised that they would never be able to outnumber Arabs in Palestine under normal conditions, and so they began to promote the idea of population 'transfer'.

PREPARING FOR THE WAR

'The Committee declares its support of the cause of the Arabs of Palestine and its willingness to work for the achievement of their legitimate aims and the safeguarding of their Just rights.

The Committee also declares that it is second to none in regretting the woes which have been inflicted upon the Jews of Europe by European dictatorial states. But the question of these Jews should not be confused with Zionism, for there can be no greater injustice and aggression than solving the problem of the Jews of Europe by another injustice, i.e., by inflicting injustice on the Arabs of Palestine of various religions and denominations.'

SPECIAL RESOLUTION CONCERNING PALESTINE, ALEXANDRIA PROTOCOL, COUNCIL OF THE LEAGUE OF ARAB STATES, OCTOBER 1944.

During the Second World War, the Jewish Agency escalated preparations for a war to take Palestine from the Arabs. Members of Hagana gained valuable training whilst serving the British on intelligence and sabotage missions in enemy territory in the Middle East. By 1941, these highly trained soldiers formed an elite military force within the Hagana, the Palmach. Hagana soldiers stationed in Europe in the war purchased or stole weapons which were smuggled into Palestine.

In 1942 Haj Amin al-Husseini, in exile from Palestine, sought support from Hitler for his ambition to be leader of the Muslim world, but Arabs in Palestine did not respond to the Mufti's radio broadcasts from Berlin in support of the Nazis. When the war ended, the League of Arab States took the lead in organising the political and military defence of Arab rights in Palestine. These preparations were hampered by a lack of unity and mutual mistrust amongst the leaders of the Arab states.

THE BATTLE FOR PALESTINE UNDER THE BRITISH

' ... [Jewish] terrorists dressed in police uniform stole a police armoured car, drove down to the Jaffa Gate, threw a bomb into a canteen, and drove back through the Mamillah Road, firing as they went. When they reached the cemetery corner on their return journey they stopped the car and threw another bomb, which killed the granite-faced constable who directed the traffic from the island.'

RICHARD GRAVES, THE BRITISH-APPOINTED MAYOR OF JERUSALEM FROM JUNE 1947 TO THE END OF THE MANDATE.[28]

As the United Nations vote on Palestine was broadcast, protests, riots and fighting between Arabs and Jews erupted in Palestine. This escalated into serious warfare over the following months. The conflict was driven by fear, anger and hatred of the other; there was no distinction between soldiers and civilians, all were regarded as the enemy. The fighters on both sides aimed to expel their enemy from as much territory as possible. The British response to the violence and disorder was piecemeal and inconsistent; their aim was to keep their own casualties to a minimum and effect their evacuation.

In the first three months of 1948, Arab guerrilla fighters were able to cut off Jewish west Jerusalem and remote Jewish settlements from outside Jewish help. But at the beginning of April 1948 the Jews went on the offensive in the Upper Galilee, driving out the inhabitants of the Arab villages in these districts and, whenever possible, blowing up their homes to prevent their return.

The Battle for Jerusalem

Arab fighters in the Jerusalem area were led by a member of the Husseini family, Abd al-Qadir al-Husseini. Arab forces had encircled the Jewish quarter of Jerusalem; control of Jerusalem centred on possession of the town of Al-Qastel. On 8th April, al-Husseini was killed trying to take the town from Jewish forces and his death devastated the Arabs of Palestine. On 9th April, LEHI and Irgun fighters entered the village of Deir Yassin, to the west of Jerusalem, and massacred 250 of the village's men, women and children. The survivors were loaded into trucks and driven around Jerusalem in an act of humiliation.

Jewish forces used the massacre at Deir Yassin to inspire fear in the Arab population so they would flee. In a futile act of revenge Arab fighters massacred a convoy of Jewish hospital workers on route to the Hadassah Hospital.

The Battle for Haifa

In Haifa, British forces maintained control of the docks area, and the routes around it, in order to effect their evacuation. They negotiated with Arab and Jewish military leaders to secure an agreed area of British control, and undertook a degree of peacekeeping during the day. At night however, fighting was intense, with both sides determined to gain control of the town. By 22nd April, the Jewish forces had taken Haifa, and large numbers of the town's Arab citizens had fled.

The Battle for Jaffa

Between 25th and 29th April, Jewish forces bombarded Jaffa with mortars, and advanced on the city. Only when the Arab position in the port of Jaffa, which had been assigned to the Arab state of Palestine in the United Nations partition plan, was on the point of collapse and most of its 90,000 inhabitants gone, did the British step in to prevent the Jews overrunning the city. They remained in control there for little more than two weeks when, on 14th May 1948 – the last day of the British Mandate – they were withdrawn, allowing the Jews to take possession of a largely deserted Jaffa.

> *We had heard about Deir Yassin, Nater and Mikvah Israel. I was armed with a gun that did not shoot. Convoys left Jaffa escorted by the British. If you did not go with the convoy, you were likely to be intercepted by the Haganah. We were young males: if we were caught, we would be shot. So, Mohammed and I decided to leave by boat. At ten o'clock in the morning, we met to take the jarrem, small boat, to the Princess Alexandra. The jarrem was carrying 50-60 people, a boat that could safely carry 40. Everyone was in a panic, it was the last boat. We were embarrassed. We still wanted to fight, so we returned to Jaffa on the same jarrem that took us to the boat. By 11:30 a.m, we were back at the club, our fortification. There was no one left defending the city. All the shooting*

was coming from the other side. Around 3pm, we saw smoke coming out of the smokestack of the boat. The boat was about to leave. Mohammed and I left our guns and ran to the last jarrem. Mohammed and I were the last to board the Princess Alexandra. We were sitting in the corridor and a Belgian sailor passed. He looked at us and asked: 'Why did you leave your country?' I didn't have an answer.'

Ibrahim Abu-Lughod[29]

On 14th May, the British Army successfully extricated the civilian administration and its garrison from war-torn Jerusalem as General Sir Alan Cunningham, the seventh and last British High Commissioner for Palestine, stepped onto a Royal Navy cruiser *HMS Euryalus* in the port of Haifa at the beginning of his journey back to Great Britain. At midnight, *HMS Euryalus* paused on the three mile limit and a band played 'Auld Lang Syne' on board the flight deck of an aircraft carrier nearby as the British Mandate came to an end. That evening David Ben Gurion, chairman of the Jewish Agency Executive, declared the establishment of the state of Israel to a packed audience in a Tel Aviv art gallery. A British enclave where a huge mountain of stores still awaited shipping back to the UK would remain in existence in Haifa until 30th June, when the Union flag was lowered for the last time and British troops sailed away.

'We thought, there was a Palestinian leadership, and there was a Partition resolution, presumably the leadership would tell the United Nations, 'all right, we are against partition, but this is our state, please help us set it up.' Instead they left things in total chaos, and people were deciding for themselves, 'should I remain in my home or would I be blown up?' This is how the people of West Jerusalem left it. I saw that because I lived the last two or three months in that area. We had our studios in the German colony in Qatamon – I left it only on the 15th of May, the end of the Mandate, after the High Commissioner had left.

So we saw that there was nobody to defend us. It was a free-for-all, I mean they were putting bombs in our area, and we were putting bombs in retaliation in their areas, so there was no security whatsoever for anybody – for the Jews or for the Palestinians. When the moment of decision came, which was after the total collapse of the British Mandate, the vacuum was filled by the Israeli forces, and not by us because we had no forces. The Arab League had managed three or four thousand volunteers, I don't know how they got them. They were totally inefficient, inept, and they did nothing except steal some automobiles here and there.'

HAZEM NUSEIBEH

AFTERMATH

'Old King Abdullah of TransJordan is in Jerusalem twice a week now: I think he hopes, the wily old thing, to snaffle Arab Palestine in the event of Partition!'

LETTER HOME FROM MEMBER OF BRITISH FORCES IN PALESTINE, 24TH AUGUST, 1947.

As the Mandate officially ended, the armies of Transjordan, Iraq, Egypt, Syria and Lebanon entered Palestine. Their overall aims were unclear, and there was no unity of command. As states just emerging from colonial rule they had been reluctant to enter into a conflict for which they were ill-prepared. Only King Abdullah of Trans-Jordan showed any enthusiasm for the task; he had secret agreements with both the Jewish Agency and Britain that he would use the British-trained Arab Legion to defend and annex the territory to the west of the River Jordan in the Partition plan. The British did not want to see an independent Palestinian state under the rule of Haj Amin al-Husseini emerge from Partition.

A British Intelligence Report for the War Office dated 22nd May 1948 assessed the relative strength of the warring sides. They described Jewish forces as possessing, 'numerical superiority, interior lines, co-ordinated command, high morale and offensive spirit'. In contrast, the Arab states, despite their expressed determination to fight for Palestine, were disunited and lacked clear military command. The numbers of fighters on each side were assessed thus:

Jews	
Hagana	70,000
Irgun	4,000
Total	*74,000*
Arabs	
Arab Liberation Army	5,000
Arab Legion	5,000
Iraq forces	2,000
Egypt	5,000
Syria	1,500
Lebanon	700
Total	*19,200*

Time will put into perspective the British work in Palestine: also, indeed, the broader contribution of Britain to the solution of Jewish problems. The Colonial Office deplores that its task has concluded in the circumstances of tragedy, disintegration and heavy loss.

COLONIAL SECRETARY'S REPORT, JUNE 1948.

Israel, the new Jewish state, was able to hold at bay the five Arab armies. Early in 1949 an armistice was signed. Israel had gained three quarters of Palestine, including much prime land that had been allocated to the Arabs in the Partition plan. The remaining land on the west bank of the River Jordan was annexed into the Kingdom of Jordan, together with Jerusalem's Old City and eastern suburbs. The only other remnant of Palestine still in Arab hands consisted of a narrow corridor of land centred on Rafah and Gaza which the Egyptian army had managed to cling to. The world now knows this finger of land as the Gaza Strip.

850,000 Palestinian Arabs had lived in the area of Palestine assigned to the Jewish state by the United Nations partition plan. By 1949, 100,000 of them, mainly in the Galilee, had managed to stay put. The rest had been driven out by Jewish forces or fled in fear for their lives, a high proportion either to the Gaza Strip or the West Bank but many more to Lebanon, Syria and Jordan. The homes and valuables they left behind were either destroyed by the Israeli Defence Forces, appropriated by Jewish residents or taken over by the Israeli authorities and sold. None of the Palestinian residents was allowed to return, although the new state of Israel opened its doors to any Jew anywhere in the world who wanted to come and live there.

'I think most people have made their peace with their Mandate memories. It's more a question of nostalgia these days: the 'good old days'. You used to say in the first years of the state, 'In the good old days when the British were in the country and the piastre had a hole in it.' The one piastre coin had a hole because the Arab women, especially Bedouin women, would carry them like treasure around their heads. I think people now remember them with nostalgia. I think if you ask people – were the British good or bad for the Jews? – most people would give you a positive answer nowadays.

There was a joke – in 1949 there were the elections for the first Knesset, and Begin's new party gained a big victory; 18 seats, I think, out of 120. Two years later there was another election for the second Knesset, and he lost half of his strength. The question was why did he win in '49? Because he had driven out the British. Why did he lose in '51? Because he had driven out the British!'

URI AVNERY

'I blame the British because they had the power to arrange the situation in a far, far better way than they did. They abandoned Palestine; they abandoned a sacred trust which was given them by the League of Nations. This does not exonerate other parties, I do not exonerate the Palestinian leaders, I do not

exonerate the United Nations itself for the Partition. The British abandoned Palestine without saying goodbye to anybody. This is not what they did when they left India. In India they handed over that part to India and the other part to Pakistan. There were ceremonies, there were raising of the flag and lowering of the flag. In the case of Palestine, they simply got out, it disintegrated. Day after day, day after day, it disintegrated, regardless of any consequences. – The British knew exactly what was going to happen, and therefore they should have behaved differently and protected the Palestinian people as a trust, and not let them just disperse as they did.'

Hazem Nuseibeh

Picture Sources

The black and white photographs were all taken from the Matson Collection of photographs of Palestine, held at the Library of Congress in Washington D.C. and available in various resolutions on the following website: http://www.loc.gov/pictures/collection/matpc/background.html

Each photograph is identified by a prefix and a number. The prefix is usually of the form LC-DIG-matpc and the numbers are those given below, specifying the original photograph from which the illustration has been taken. So to find the original of the Frontispiece, for example, search for 'LC-DIG-matpc 10612' on the Library of Congress website. Sometimes the original has been cropped, for the purposes of the book.

P. 55 Sir Herbert Samuel 00730
P. 69 Tel Aviv beach 11997
P. 71 The Army in Jerusalem 15731
P. 74 Arab women protesting 15738
P. 75 British Police dog 16586
P. 77 Arabs at Abu Ghosh 18053
P. 82 Lydda house demolition 18126
P. 86 Loyalty meeting 20708
P. 87 King David Hotel explosion 12970
P. 93 Anglo-American Inquiry 12890

NOTES

Note: All 'CO' references are to Cabinet Office papers in the National Archive, London.

1 McCarthy, Justin, *The Population of Palestine*, Columbia University Press, New York, 1988, p. 37.

2 Campos, Michelle U. 'Ottoman Brothers' from *Ottoman Brothers – Muslims, Christians, and Jews in Early Twentieth –Century Palestine*, Stanford University Press, California, 2011.

3 Quoted in Baldensperger, Philip. *The Immovable East*, Pitman Publishing, London, 1913.

4 Thompson, William McClure. *The Land and the Book*, Harper & Brothers, New York, 1859.

5 Wilson, Charles Thomas. *Peasant Life in the Holy Land*, J. Murray, London, 1906.

6 Conder, Claude Reigner. *Tent Work in Palestine*, R. Bentley & Son, London, 1878.

7 Palestine Exploration Fund, Survey of Western Palestine, 1882–88

8 Furlonge, Geoffrey W. *Palestine is my Country – the Story of Musa Alami*, Praeger Publishers, New York, 1969.

9 Palestine Exploration Fund, Survey of Western Palestine, 1882.

10 Weizmann's report on his appearance before the Peace Conference, 27th February 1919. Quoted in *Rise of Israel*, Vol 10, p. 177, Garland Publishing Inc, 1987.

11 Churchill papers, CHAR 16/18.

12 A.J. Balfour in letter to U.S. Secretary of State, Charles E. Hughes, 13th January 1922.

13 List of members of the Zionist Commission enclosed with a letter from the British Headquarters of the Military Administration in Cairo dated 21st April 1920.

14 Cabinet paper 'The Future of Palestine', 27th July 1923. CO 733/58.

15 Keith-Roache, Edward, *Pasha of Jerusalem: Memoirs of a District Commissioner Under the British Mandate*, Palgrave Macmillan, London, 1994.

16 Horne, Edward. *A Job Well Done*, Anchor Press, Sussex, 1982.

17 Akram Zu'aiter Private Papers, IPS.

18 Koestler, Arthur, *Promise and Fulfilment: Palestine 1917–1949* (1949), Pages 34–35.

19 Quoted in Segev, Tom, *One Palestine Complete,* Metropolitan Books, 2000

20 Minutes of a telephone conversation between the prime minister and Weizmann from the Zionist office at 9.30 p.m., quoted in Rose, N.A., *The Gentile Zionists*, Frank Cass, London, 1973, p. 26.

21 *Filastin wal-Isti'mar al-Jadid,* (Palestine and the New Colonisation) A poem about the Zionist threat to Palestine, printed in al-Nafa'is al-Asriyya, 1910.

22 Zua'itar Private Papers, Institute of Palestine Studies, Beirut.

23 CO 733/310/1

24 CO 733/371/2

25 Edwardes, O.S. *Palestine: Land of Broken Promises,* Dorothy Crisp & Co, 1946, p. 110.

26 Unpublished diaries, c.1950, Institute of Palestine Studies, Beirut

27 CO 537/2332

28 Extract for 12th January 1948 from Graves, Richard Massie. *Experiment in Anarchy*, V. Gollancz, London, 1949.

29 *Resistance, Exile and Return, Conversations with Hisham Ahmed-Fararjeh,* Ibrahim Abu-Lughod Institute of International Studies, 2003.